Blackburn
College

Classical World series

Aristophanes and His Theatre of the Absurd P. Cartledge
Art and the Romans A. Haward
Athens and Sparta S. Todd
Athens Under the Tyrants J. Smith
Attic Orators M. Edwards
Augustan Rome A. Wallace-Hadrill
Cicero and the End of the Roman Republic T. Wiedemann
Classical Archaeology in the Field L. Bowkett et al.
Classical Epic: Homer and Virgil R. Jenkyns
Democracy in Classical Athens C. Carey
Environment and the Classical World P. Jeskins
Greece and the Persians J. Sharwood Smith
Greek and Roman Historians T. Duff
Greek and Roman Medicine H. King
Greek Architecture R. Tomlinson
Greek Tragedy: an introduction M. Baldock
Julio-Claudian Emperors: AD 14-70 T. Wiedemann
Lucretius and the Didactic Epic M. Gale
Morals and Values in Ancient Greece J. Ferguson
Mycenaean World K. & D. Wardle
Plato's Republic and the Greek Enlightenment H. Lawson-Tancred
Plays of Euripides J. Morwood
Plays of Sophocles A. Garvie
Political Life in the City of Rome J. Patterson
Religion and the Greeks R. Garland
Religion and the Romans K. Dowden
Roman Architecture M. Thorpe
Roman Britain S. Hill & S. Ireland
Roman Satirists and their Masks S. Morton Braund
Slavery in Classical Greece N. Fisher
Women in Classical Athens S. Blundell

Classical World Series

THE PLAYS
OF
SOPHOCLES

A.F. Garvie

Bristol Classical Press

First published in 2005 by
Bristol Classical Press
an imprint of
Gerald Duckworth & Co. Ltd.
90-93 Cowcross Street, London EC1M 6BF
Tel: 020 7490 7300
Fax: 020 7490 0080
inquiries@duckworth-publishers.co.uk
www.ducknet.co.uk

A catalogue record for this book is available
from the British Library

ISBN 1 85399 680 7

Printed and bound in Great Britain by
Antony Rowe Ltd

Contents

Preface

I owe a debt of gratitude to colleagues at Glasgow and to many students, both undergraduate and postgraduate, with whom it has been a pleasure to study and to discuss Sophocles over many years. It has been a particular privilege to supervise, and to learn from, the PhD theses of Vayos Liapis on 'Nothing that is not Zeus: the unknowability of the gods and limits of human knowledge in Sophoclean tragedy', and of Marigo Alexopoulou, whose work on *nostos* in Greek tragedy has helped me greatly with my chapter on *Women of Trachis*.

As always, I thank my wife, Jane, and my daughter, Margaret Haynes, for their patience in correcting obscurities and inconsistencies in expression and in presentation, and my son, David, for his help and advice in all matters pertaining to information technology.

I am greatly indebted to Michael Gunningham, who, as Series Editor in 2002, invited me to write this book, and to Deborah Blake, Editorial Director at Duckworth, for all her care and helpfulness.

I acknowledge with thanks the kind permission of Oxbow Books to use for the chapter on *Ajax* my translation of that play which was published in 1998 by Aris & Phillips as *Sophocles Ajax: edited with introduction, translation and commentary*.

A.F. Garvie
University of Glasgow

Introduction

The format of this book is based largely on that of James Morwood's *The Plays of Euripides* (2002) in the same series. I have kept to a bare minimum references to the secondary literature on Sophocles, and I have supplied line references to the text of the plays only where it seemed to be essential. I have tried as far as possible to avoid technical terms. The scale of this volume has precluded any attempt to deal with the lyric metres of the Chorus' songs and of those passages in which a chorus and an actor join in a lyric exchange. The reader, however, should remember that, although the chorus-leader may engage in spoken dialogue with a character, the chorus itself never speaks, but always sings and dances – a vital element of Greek tragedy which is largely lost to a modern audience or reader. I should like to have said more about the staging of the plays, but again space has not permitted.

In the course of his long life (he was about ninety when he died in 406 BC) Sophocles is thought to have written about 120 plays. His first victory in the competition for best tragedian of the year was in 468 BC. This may also have been his first production. In terms of victories he was the most successful of the three great fifth-century Athenian tragedians. Only seven of his tragedies, together with a large number of fragments, survive intact. This volume deals with the seven plays in the order in which they may have been first produced. But only two dates are certain: *Philoctetes* was produced in 409 BC, *Oedipus at Colonus* posthumously in 401. A story in Plutarch (first to second centuries AD) which connects *Antigone* with Sophocles' appointment as a general in 441/40 would point to 442 as the date of that play, but it may not be reliable. *Oedipus the King* has usually been dated to the early 420s, largely on the dubious grounds that the plague with which the play begins must have been based on the real plague in Athens in 431. Most, but not all, scholars believe, on grounds of style and structure, that *Ajax*, *Women of Trachis* and *Antigone* can be grouped as the earliest surviving plays, and that they all belong probably in the 440s, but there is less agreement about the order in which the three were produced. *Electra* is usually believed to come between *Oedipus the King* and *Philoctetes*, probably between 420 and 410. All of this uncertainty renders very hazardous any attempt to trace a development in Sophocles' dramatic technique or tragic thinking, and no such attempt will be made in these essays. A single papyrus find could upset many cherished views.

The translations, which are my own, are based, for the most part, on the 1990 Oxford Classical Text of H. Lloyd-Jones and N.G. Wilson.

Ajax

After the death of the Greek hero Achilles at Troy, Ajax committed suicide because Achilles' armour was awarded not to him but to Odysseus, as the next best warrior after Achilles. The story was known to Homer, who in *Odyssey* 11 presents a memorable encounter between Odysseus and Ajax in the Underworld, with the latter refusing his enemy's offer of reconciliation. It was treated more fully in some of the lost poems of the post-Homeric Epic Cycle, and it was a popular subject in art from the seventh century onwards. In Sophocles' version Ajax commits suicide, not only because of the dishonour done to him by the refusal to award him Achilles' arms, but because he has failed in his attempt to avenge himself by killing the commanders of the army, Agamemnon and Menelaus.

A modern audience or reader might be expected to find it difficult to sympathise, or identify, with a man who, for apparently selfish reasons, behaves so disloyally towards his comrades, and who, when his attempt is foiled by the goddess Athena, regrets not his murderous intentions but only his failure to carry them out. For the ancient audience too, living in a democracy in which self-centred 'heroic' individualists represented a threat to civic cohesion, Ajax's behaviour must have seemed problematic. At the same time even in fifth-century Athens such individualists were needed and admired. Ajax belongs to a long line of Sophoclean heroes who, in one way or another, are isolated from their community, who fall because they insist on remaining true to themselves, and whom, because of their determination, we are invited to pity and admire. Ajax embodies, albeit in an extreme form, the code of the Homeric warrior, for whom honour depended on success, and failure led to disgrace.

The original audience also took it for granted that one should do good to one's friends, but as much harm as possible to one's enemies (see pp. 40, 79). His enemies will naturally object to his behaviour, and we may continue to have doubts about it, but it is broadly true that 'Sophocles does not judge the morality of Ajax's action in trying to attack the Greek leaders' (March 1991-3). Moreover, as the play progresses, increasing stress is laid on Ajax's positive qualities, rather than on the negative aspects of his attempted revenge. In a very real sense the play presents the rehabilitation of Ajax, as we see him restored to his status as a great man. For the Athenian audience Ajax was a hero in the Greek sense of that word, a great man who after death was elevated to a status between human and divine, and who was worshipped with a state-cult. Not much is made of this for most of the play, but the cult is certainly implied at 1176-7 and in the tableau in the final scene, in which Ajax's son Eurysaces clings in supplication to his father's corpse.

We are introduced to Ajax first through the words of his enemies, the goddess Athena and her favourite, Odysseus, who had robbed him of his prize. Athena exults in her triumph over her enemy; she has driven him mad, so that he has slaughtered sheep and cattle, under the delusion that they are Agamemnon and Menelaus, and is now about to torture a sheep, thinking that it is Odysseus. She proposes to call Ajax out of his hut so that Odysseus can enjoy the spectacle of the mad Ajax and laugh at him in his misfortune. In the final words of the scene she draws what too many scholars have taken to be the moral of the play: 'it is the sound-minded (*sophrones*) whom the gods love, while they hate the wicked' (132-3). 'Sound-mindedness' (*sophrosyne*) implies moderation, modesty, self-control, prudence, common-sense, discipline, and these tame virtues certainly do not characterise Ajax. But is this really the reason for his fall? And in what sense is he 'wicked'?

Athena seems to mean little more than that the gods honour those who pay them proper respect.

The word *hybris* is often in antithesis with *sophrosyne*. It is applied to any kind of outrageous behaviour, for example ridicule, which is calculated to bring dishonour on another person. The term occurs more often in *Ajax* than in any other surviving play of Sophocles. It is not used in this scene, but the laughter of one's enemies is often seen as a form of *hybris*, and that laughter will be a recurring theme in the play. In inviting Odysseus to laugh at Ajax Athena is thus in effect inviting him to commit *hybris*, which surely undermines the supposed pious moral that she expounds. So too does her statement that the alternation of fortune affects the good and the bad alike. Even more significant is the response of Odysseus, traditionally Ajax's greatest enemy (78). One is expected to do good to one's friends, and to harm one's enemies. But Odysseus surprises us; he declines to laugh, but rather pities Ajax, on the grounds (121-6) that they share a common humanity. Odysseus' sympathy is much more attractive than the triumphalism of the goddess, and it prepares us for the final scene of the play, in which it is Odysseus who persuades Agamemnon to allow Ajax's burial. The rehabilitation of Ajax has already begun.

For most of the rest of the play we see Ajax through the eyes, and in the presence, of his friends, who are naturally sympathetic to him – the Chorus of sailors from his island of Salamis (part of Athens since the sixth century), his concubine Tecmessa, and, after his suicide, his half-brother Teucer. To these we must add his little son, Eurysaces, to whom, in a moving speech (545-82) he bequeaths the great shield (*sakos*) for which he is famous in the *Iliad*, and from which the boy derives his name. It is in these central scenes that most of the occurrences of the term *hybris* are to be found. The Chorus uses it in its entrance-song (*parodos*) at 151-3, 196-9 as it envisages the laughter of Ajax's enemies at his misfortune, Ajax himself at 560-1 when he forecasts their treatment of Eurysaces, Teucer later at 971. In all of them the word is used by

Ajax and his supporters of his enemies' behaviour, and no one has yet described *his* behaviour in these terms.

What worries his friends is the suspicion that Ajax is about to commit suicide. When he returns to sanity they do their best to comfort him, and to make him see sense, but, as always in Sophocles, the hero refuses to be persuaded or to compromise or to yield. The word 'yield' is a keyword in most of Sophocles' plays, always put in the mouths of minor characters, the ordinary people, but it is what the hero cannot bring himself to do. The strongest pressure is put on him by the modest and faithful Tecmessa, who, in a speech carefully calculated to appeal to his sense of honour and fear of disgrace (485-524), challenges Ajax's view of the obligations of the great man, insisting that it should include the notions of gratitude and responsibility to his dependants. But for Ajax it is his failure and consequent disgrace alone that matter, and it is clear that suicide is for him the only solution: 'The noble man should either live well or die well. You have heard my whole account' (479-80).

Of Ajax's four great monologues the most famous, and the most difficult to interpret, is that at 646-92, in which he appears to have changed his mind about committing suicide. Much of it has the ring of a soliloquy in which he is talking to himself, but the many ambiguities in the language show that he is conscious of the presence of Tecmessa and the Chorus. He has after all, he says, been softened, like a woman, by Tecmessa's words, and 'I shall go to the bathing-place and the meadows by the shore, to wash away my defilement and escape from the heavy anger of the goddess'. Just as in the natural world, the principle of alternation reigns: winter gives way to summer, night to day, and sleep to wakefulness, so he too will change and yield, and he will learn to be *sophron*. 'We shall know in future to yield to the gods, and we shall learn to reverence the sons of Atreus'. The exaggerated language of at least this sentence should put us on our guard as to his sincerity. He goes on to say that friends change into enemies, and enemies into friends.

The speech has been the subject of intense debate. Some have argued that Ajax means exactly what he says; he really has changed in character, he has learnt *sophrosyne*, and no longer means to kill himself. But it then becomes impossible to explain why he does in fact commit suicide later in the play. For others the ambiguous language shows a conscious intention to deceive. His hearers certainly *are* deceived. After his exit the Chorus sings a joyous ode, of a kind which frequently in Sophocles comes immediately before the catastrophe. On the other hand, the language of the speech is so beautiful that it is hard to believe that it is all expended on a lie. I have argued in my 1998 edition that Ajax does feel intellectually the attraction of *sophrosyne* and submission, and that he is tempted to give in to it, but that emotionally he resists. The world which he describes is not one in which he feels that he has a place. The Sophoclean hero must remain true to himself, and we admire him for doing so. A modest, humble Ajax would be a disappointment to the audience.

The Chorus' happy ode is followed by the arrival of a messenger from Teucer, who has come to report the warning of the prophet Calchas that Ajax will be saved only if he can be kept inside his hut for the remainder of the day; tomorrow Athena's anger will have passed. Immediately the anxiety returns. The Messenger reports two occasions in the past on which Ajax angered Athena by his foolish boasting. This is certainly consistent with Ajax as we have seen him. Critics who look for a simple moral seize on these occasions as providing the reason for Ajax's fall. Avoid such arrogance and impiety, and you will live a happy and successful life. But we have already seen reason to suspect Athena's judgement, and it is hardly credible that Ajax falls because of something that happened long ago, and is not related to anything in the action of the play itself. How too can we take seriously a divine anger that will last only for today? The point of all this is dramatic; it increases our sense of urgency. Since Ajax has already left the hut, Tecmessa and the Chorus all depart, too late, in a frenzied search for him, leaving the stage empty for Ajax's final great soliloquy before his death. Such a departure by a chorus in the middle of a play is rare in tragedy. But Sophocles wants Ajax to die alone, isolated in his death as in his life.

According to the usual view, for Ajax's suicide the scene shifts to the lonely meadows on the shore to which Ajax has told us that he was going (654-5). Scullion is alone in arguing that there is no change of scene at all. Whether the audience actually sees Ajax fall on his sword, a rare event on the tragic stage, or whether the suicide is somehow concealed, is a much-debated question. If, as seems likely, the former alternative is correct, the corpse has by some means to be later removed, and a dummy substituted, in order to allow the actor playing Ajax to reappear as Teucer in the final scenes, in which three actors are required.

It has sometimes been said that the scenes which follow the suicide are anticlimactic, because with the removal of the main character the real interest of the play has gone. It was once common to label as a 'diptych play' the kind of drama which, like *Women of Trachis* and *Antigone*, seemed to fall in this way into two parts. If the label implies that a play is badly constructed and lacking in dramatic unity, it is better avoided. The question is whether *Ajax* does in fact lack dramatic unity. The chief concern from now on is the refusal of the sons of Atreus, Agamemnon and Menelaus, to allow Ajax to be buried. It is not enough to argue that for an ancient audience a proper burial for the dead was a matter of supreme importance. So it was, as we shall see again in *Antigone*, but so it is also in more modern societies. What matters is the audience-expectation that Sophocles has built up throughout the play. Ajax has died true to his own values, superbly confident of his own pre-eminence. And this pre-eminence has been acknowledged by his friends. But that is not enough. It has to be acknowledged by others too.

The first, sorrowful, reaction to his death is that of Tecmessa and the Chorus, and of the long-awaited Teucer when he at last arrives. Throughout all this we are kept waiting for the reaction of his enemies. Ajax's excellence was denied by those who, in his eyes, robbed him of Achilles' arms, and his failure to take vengeance has brought him into disgrace. Now his rehabilitation, and in a sense his restoration to society, depend upon a proper funeral. That he understood this on the point of death is clear from his final speech (827-30), 'that [Teucer] may be the first to lift me up when I have fallen round this freshly-sprinkled sword, and that I may not be spotted first by any of my enemies and cast out as a prey for the dogs and birds'. The original audience may have been divided as to whether the suicide was by itself a way for Ajax to restore his honour. Belfiore argues that for many Greeks male (as opposed to female) suicide was not a noble or heroic death. Without his burial his suicide may turn out to be an empty gesture. Throughout the final scenes all our concentration is still on Ajax, his corpse the centrepiece of the action. The powerful tableau contrasts with the earlier tableau in which we saw Ajax sitting in the midst of the slaughtered animals.

Now, for the first time since the prologue, we see him through the eyes of his enemies. His friends' expectation that they will laugh and treat him with *hybris* (see pp. 12-13) is duly fulfilled when first Menelaus and then Agamemnon appear. They are adamant that Ajax is to be left unburied on the ground. Neither is impressive, and the contrast between his true greatness and their blustering could hardly be greater. Menelaus' arguments are in themselves not unsound, but he starts, in the eyes of an Athenian audience, from the disadvantage of being a Spartan. That he is in favour of *sophrosyne*, and of the need for discipline in an army and a state, is not in itself surprising, but for him it means little more than the duty of 'a bad man' and a 'commoner' (1071-2, a grossly inadequate description of Ajax) to obey his rulers. It does not help his case that we are reminded of the words of Athena at 132-3 (see p. 12).

Menelaus is the first to describe Ajax's behaviour in terms of *hybris*, which in itself is not unreasonable, given that he was his intended victim. But the effect is spoilt by his boast that it is now his turn to 'think big', i.e. in effect to commit *hybris* against his enemy. After his departure the Chorus sings a melancholy ode in which it contrasts the misery of life in camp at Troy with the pleasures of life at home on Salamis. These two environments have made Ajax what he is, and throughout the play they are constantly in the thoughts of both Ajax and the Chorus.

Agamemnon, like his brother, and probably played by the same actor, is a bully. Unlike him, he at least pays some attention to Ajax's services at Troy, but he does so only to decry them, on the grounds that Ajax is no better than himself. Sophocles' audience may well disagree. He gratuitously insults Teucer, who, says Agamemnon, is committing *hybris* (1258) and ought to learn *sophrosyne*; he is a barbarian and a slave. Teucer was in fact the son of Telamon and Hesione, daughter of Laomedon king of Troy. He is certainly not a slave, and he has been speaking normal Greek. Teucer, who is probably played by the same actor as Ajax, does his best to defend his half-brother. In his attitude to his friends he is more attractive than was Ajax, and on the whole he has the better of the verbal argument with both Menelaus and Agamemnon. Nevertheless, he descends himself to the petty level of his opponents, and, the crucial point, ultimately he is unsuccessful in his attempt to secure the burial.

It is the intervention of Ajax's enemy Odysseus that provides the breakthrough. To Ajax's friends this comes as a complete surprise. It is less of a surprise to the audience, which has already noted the reaction of Odysseus in the prologue. But, since then, we have seen him only through the eyes of his enemies, and we have come to think of him as an unscrupulous villain, ready to use any means to gain his ends. In his encounter with Agamemnon he does indeed display his traditional cleverness, but now uses it to persuade Agamemnon to allow the burial, in accordance with the laws of the gods that all men should be buried. Odysseus pays little attention to what Ajax has done. All that matters is what he was, and the common humanity which both men shared. 'The man was my enemy, but he was noble once' (1355), and 'his excellence prevails with me more than his enmity' (1357). Odysseus has learnt the lesson of alternation: he forgets his enmity, and becomes Ajax's friend. But Agamemnon never understands. He yields only because Odysseus persuades him to put his desire to help his friend (Odysseus) above his wish to harm his enemy. The play ends with the procession in which the corpse is duly carried off for burial. And 'Teucer's final words are an invitation to the audience to join imaginatively and emotionally in the funeral' (March 1991-3).

In one sense the play has a happy ending. Ajax has got what he wanted, and his reputation has been restored. Odysseus has acknowledged him, in the final testimony to his greatness, as 'the most excellent man of all the Argives ... except for Achilles' (1340-1). And yet the closure is somehow incomplete. We cannot quite forget Ajax's disloyalty to the army, and much in his character has been unattractive – his gloating over the details of his supposed vengeance on his enemies, his treatment of the faithful Tecmessa, his refusal to listen to his friends. Ajax's excellence has been recognised, and we admire him for it. But we do not have to like him. Much more attractive is the character of the flexible Odysseus. It is ironical that for his burial Ajax has had to depend, not on his friends, but on his enemy, and that he secures it only because that enemy has become a friend. We recall the words of Ajax about this kind of alternation (679-82), and we feel that it is one that he could never accept for himself. Just as Agamemnon refuses to become the friend of Ajax, so the rigid Ajax could never acknowledge Odysseus as his friend.

Even the final procession is somehow flawed. The fact that anyone from the army is invited to participate in the funeral marks, in a sense, Ajax's (and the Chorus') reintegration into the community. But Teucer, despite his gratitude to Odysseus, in deference to Ajax allows him only a restricted part in the ceremony. Odysseus departs before the procession begins, and Agamemnon and Menelaus will certainly not be present. As so often, Sophocles combines optimism with pessimism. The gods provide little comfort. Athena makes no appearance at the end. One feels that, like Ajax himself, she would not have understood Odysseus' magnanimity.

If, finally, we ask why Ajax falls, the answer is not that it is because he has done anything wrong. Rather, he is ruined because of the qualities for which we admire him. If he had not been the kind of man he was, he would not have fallen.

Women of Trachis

Like Aeschylus' *Persians* and *Agamemnon*, *Women of Trachis* presents the tragedy of a long-awaited, but ultimately unhappy, homecoming. At the beginning of the play Heracles, the mortal son of Zeus, after completing the Labours forced upon him by Eurystheus, has been abroad for fifteen months, but nobody at home in Trachis knows where he is. Most of the play concentrates on the effect of his absence on his wife Deianeira, and we are kept waiting until the final scene for Heracles' arrival on the stage. We are two-thirds of the way through the play before Deianeira makes her final exit, while Heracles is on stage for only about the last quarter of the play. The result of this is that, as in *Antigone* (see pp. 37-8), there is no single dominant character, and it is idle to argue over who is 'the hero' of the play. The tragedy concerns a relationship between two characters, husband and wife, both of them ruined by the power of Eros (Love). Heracles more closely resembles the 'typical' Sophoclean hero, but it is Deianeira who has the bigger part, and more lines to speak. Not surprisingly, this play, like *Ajax* and *Antigone*, has been unhelpfully labelled by some critics as a 'diptych' play (see p. 16), with its first part devoted to Deianeira's tragedy, the second to that of Heracles. It certainly displays a structural unity. From the very beginning we look forward to Heracles' return, and that return will form the dramatic climax at the end. The effect of his absence on Deianeira, and the steps which she takes to prepare for Heracles' return, will make that return all the more horrific.

The minor characters too have their role to play in the tragedy: the Nurse, whom we meet in the prologue, as Deianeira's faithful supporter; the equally sympathetic Chorus of young Trachinian women, from whom the play takes its title; the Messenger; the Herald Lichas; Iole, brought back by Lichas to be Heracles' concubine; and Hyllus, the son of Heracles and Deianeira. Lichas and Hyllus in particular will be involved in the tragedy. The whole play presents a tangle of misunderstandings. Good people set out to do what they think is right, but their actions have the opposite effect to what they intended. Deianeira, in particular, destroys the husband whom she loves and yearns to see. And behind it all is the gradual revelation of the mysterious oracles, which the characters misinterpret, and the enigmatic attitude of the gods to the suffering of the human participants.

All the other surviving plays of Sophocles begin with a prologue in the form of dialogue. Here Deianeira enters with the Nurse, but her opening speech of 48 lines is not addressed to her; it is a soliloquy addressed in effect to the audience, Euripides' preferred method of beginning his plays. The obvious function of the monologue is to set the scene for the audience. More important, it introduces us at the very beginning to Deianeira's state of mind. Her opening lines present the theme of alternation in human fortunes, as important in this play as in *Ajax*. But she herself has been uniformly unhappy, and the keynote of her unhappiness is marriage. Before her marriage to Heracles she had experienced the attentions of the repulsive river-god Achelous. It was Heracles who fought the god and saved her from that marriage, and thus brought her joy. Married now to Heracles she ought to be happy, but instead she is afraid. Her husband is always away from home, and, since for the past fifteen months no message has arrived from him, she does not know what has happened to him. So the play begins with forebodings which centre on Deianeira's marriage, forebodings which are intensified when at the end of her speech she mentions a tablet which Heracles had left with her on his departure; 'I often pray to the gods that trouble will not result from my receiving it' (47-8). Our curiosity is aroused, but we shall have to wait for a little while to learn more about this tablet.

The Nurse advises Deianeira to send her son Hyllus to see if he can find news of his father. Hyllus conveniently arrives at this very moment, and Deianeira explains her trouble to him. He has heard rumours that Heracles, after being enslaved to a Lydian woman, Omphale, is now, or will soon be, in Euboea, making war on Eurytus. Deianeira tells him about the oracles which predicted that Heracles would either die, or, if he managed to complete his present task, would henceforth have a happy life. Deianeira takes this to mean that, if Hyllus finds his father still alive, all will be well. Only later will it be revealed that there is no real alternative: it is death itself that will bring peace to Heracles. Why did she not tell Hyllus about the oracles before? If it was to spare him from anxiety, this is the first instance in the play of someone acting with the best of intentions but getting it wrong. If Hyllus had known about the oracles he would have gone long ago to find his father.

In its entrance-song the Chorus picks up the burning question, 'where is Heracles?' Deianeira yearns for him. The word for 'yearning' (the noun is *pothos*, the verb *potheo*), used twice in the same stanza (103-7), emphasises the main theme that runs right through the first part of the play. The Chorus tries to console Deianeira. As with the cyclic rhythm of night and day, of sea and stars, so Heracles' troubles should give way to joy. So Heracles may have had his troubles, but up till now some god has always kept him from death. And when was Zeus unmindful of his own children? What part will the gods play in what is about to happen? And can we be so confident that for Heracles there will be an alternation from trouble to happiness, the alternation which Deianeira has already denied in her own case (Easterling)?

At the beginning of the following episode Deianeira tells the Chorus more about the tablet, the significance of which is becoming clearer and clearer. Again we hear that the period of fifteen months is crucial: at the end of it Heracles is fated either to die or to live henceforth a painless life. That time has now arrived. The mood is one of pessimism. When Heracles gave her the tablet, it was as if he were already dead, and he made arrangements for the division of his estate. It is not surprising that Deianeira fears the worst, that she is about to lose her husband, the 'best' of all men (177).

The arrival of a messenger, garlanded to show that he brings good news, provides a dramatic contrast of mood. 'Lady, Deianeira,' he begins, 'I shall be the first of messengers to release you from your fear.' Heracles will soon be safely home, or so the Messenger has heard from the herald Lichas, who is on his way to give the news in full. Immediately Deianeira moves from pessimism to joy. But the audience perhaps wonders why it needs both the Messenger and Lichas to bring the happy news, and we suspect that the joy will be short-lived. We have been waiting for Heracles, but first, as the Messenger remains on stage, we have to wait for Lichas, while the Chorus sings a joyous song of thanksgiving to the gods. At 207, according to one interpretation of the difficult Greek, the house is said to be waiting for a marriage. If this is correct, the Chorus is thinking of the reunion of husband and wife as a kind of remarriage. We shall soon learn that Heracles has in mind a different marriage.

Lichas at last appears, bringing with him a group of female prisoners. He begins by confirming the good news that Heracles is alive, and explains that he is in Euboea sacrificing to Zeus. Deianeira is curious about the prisoners, and shows some pity for them. But at first the theme is not developed. Instead, we hear from Lichas about what Heracles has been doing – how for a year he was a slave in Lydia, a punishment from Zeus because he had deceitfully killed Iphitus, the son of Eurytus, king in Euboea. It was in revenge for this, says Lichas, that Heracles attacked Eurytus' city, and the prisoners have come from it. Now Deianeira, who has waited so long for her husband, has to wait again until he completes his sacrifices.

She again expresses her happiness, but this time qualifies it immediately with the thought that happiness cannot last; one must always expect alternations in human affairs. Given the nature of Greek tragedy, unhappy people rarely believe that their misery will ever end. With that thought in mind she turns again to the prisoners, who must once have been free and happy. One of them in particular strikes her by her beauty and her noble bearing, and she pities her the most. She tries to speak to her, but Iole does not answer. Lichas explains that she has not uttered a word, but has wept continuously, since she was enslaved. There are already three speaking actors on the stage, and Greek tragedy did not permit a fourth. Iole is therefore played by a mute. But, at the same time, the silence of the character who is to play so large a part in the tragedy is extraordinarily effective. We never hear her express her own point of view, but here her plight is revealed to us through the sympathetic words of the woman who does not want to add to her pain, but who will be destroyed by her.

Lichas takes the captives into the house, but Deianeira is detained by the Messenger. Now we learn why Sophocles required both Messenger and Lichas. We probably thought that the former's role was finished, but his intervention now is all-important, in that once more it completely reverses the mood. The Messenger reveals that Lichas has not told the truth. Heracles' real motive for attacking Eurytus' city was his love for Iole. He was inflamed by desire (*pothos* 368, cf. 431), the very word used by Deianeira of her own feelings for her husband. Now she is reduced again to utter misery, made all the worse when Lichas returns to be questioned by the Messenger, who reminds him of his statement that Heracles has brought Iole home to be his wife (or concubine – her legal status is never entirely clear). Seaford has shown that many things in this play suggest a perversion of normal marriage-ritual. Here the audience may think of the traditional procession of the bride and bridegroom to the latter's house. But it is Deianeira, Heracles' existing wife, not his mother, who stands in front of the house to welcome the bride, like Clytaemnestra welcoming Cassandra in Aeschylus' *Agamemnon*.

In a long speech Deianeira, a model of *sophrosyne*, displays remarkable magnanimity. After another reference to the theme of alternation, she goes on to talk about the power of Eros ('Love'). She cannot blame either Heracles or Iole. All she wants is to know the truth. She has put up with Heracles' previous sexual conquests, and she pities Iole. We have no real reason to doubt her sincerity. Lichas confesses. Heracles had not told him to conceal the truth, but he did so because he did not want to hurt Deianeira. Lichas is no villain, but his attempt to do right has gone horribly wrong. He ends his speech with the bitter thought that Heracles, who in everything else had proved himself supreme, has been completely defeated by his love for Iole. After declaring that she has no intention of fighting against the gods, Deianeira, with Lichas, retires into the house to prepare gifts, as yet unspecified, for Lichas to carry to Heracles, and thus sets in motion the whole inevitable course of the tragedy.

The power of Love, a common theme in Greek tragedy (see p. 35) is the subject of the Chorus' next song. It recalls the fight between the monstrous Achelous and Heracles, each eager to win Deianeira for his bride. Aphrodite, goddess of love, was the umpire, while Deianeira sat waiting for the victor. All her life since then she has been waiting.

The next episode begins with her return to the stage with a sealed casket which contains the gift that she has devised. She has become less sympathetic to Iole, whom she thinks of as already 'yoked' to Heracles (contrast 309 where she judged Iole to be inexperienced in such matters). She finds it hard to tolerate the thought of sharing Heracles' bed with Iole. Still, she is not angry with Heracles, for whom it is natural to prefer a younger woman. Her gift to him is a love-potion or aphrodisiac to restore his love for her. She has smeared a robe with the blood of the Centaur Nessus, like Achelous a monster from Heracles' past. Nessus was carrying Deianeira across a river, and, when he tried to rape her, Heracles killed him, but before he died Nessus gave her drops of his blood, promising that if she used it Heracles would never prefer any other woman to herself. But the blood was infected with the poison of the Hydra (yet another monster from the past), in which Heracles had dipped his arrows. Deianeira certainly does not want to harm her husband, and she is uneasy: 'May I never come to know or learn about deeds of wicked daring; I hate those women who indulge in them' (582-3). When she does understand her folly it will be too late. The Chorus approves, but Deianeira, in asking it to keep her secret, already shows some misgivings about the morality of her action: 'If it is in the dark that you act shamefully, you will never fall in shame' (596-7). Lichas enters to receive his instructions, and Deianeira, who had criticised him for concealing the truth, now herself misleads him as to her motive for sending the robe: she wants Heracles, she says, to be well dressed when he comes home and sacrifices to the gods. She ends the episode by ordering Lichas not to tell Heracles of her yearning (*pothos*) for him until she knows if it is reciprocated.

So Deianeira has taken the fatal step which will ruin both Heracles and herself. Her *sophrosyne* will not save her. She is 'a modest wife of conventional virtue who performs a daring deed. She acts out of character ... she makes the inevitable disastrous mistake' (Winnington-Ingram). Or, as Segal (1995) puts it, 'endowed with the soul of a Penelope, she executes, unwittingly, the deed of a Clytaemnestra or a Medea'.

The Chorus, left alone, sings the kind of happy ode which Sophocles likes to place immediately before disaster strikes (see p. 15). It waits in joyful expectation for the return of Heracles who is hurrying home bearing all the spoils of his valour (*arete*). Instead of Heracles, however, it is once more Deianeira who appears, in a state of apprehension that contrasts with the joy of the ode. She is afraid that, although she meant well, she may have committed a great wrong. The tuft of wool with which she had anointed the robe crumbled away when it met the sunlight. By the end of her long account her apprehension has turned to certainty: 'I see that I have done a terrible deed' (706). Too late she realises the truth: Nessus had deceived her, and the 'love-potion' is in fact a deadly poison, which kills everything that it touches. No longer indecisive, she resolves to die with Heracles; for life is intolerable for a woman who is not evil to have it said of her that she *is* evil (721-2). She remains uncomforted by the Chorus-leader's urging that she should not abandon hope, and by the argument that people make allowances for those who do wrong unintentionally.

All Deianeira's fears are soon justified by the entry of Hyllus, the third person in the play to come with news of the long-awaited Heracles. He begins by denouncing his mother, whom now he hates, before launching into his long story of how glad he had been to find his father whom he had yearned to see (*pothos*). But then Lichas had arrived with the robe, and we hear at length of the disastrous effect of the poison on Heracles. As it began to consume him he blamed the unfortunate Lichas and killed him instantly, the first, innocent, victim of Deianeira's plan. He cursed his marriage to Deianeira who had ruined him. Her gift has had the opposite result to that which she intended.

Hyllus has brought his tortured father home. 'You will see him immediately, either alive or newly dead' (805-6). Once more we are encouraged to look forward to Heracles' homecoming, but now it will clearly be a very different homecoming from that which was expected. Hyllus too curses Deianeira. He wants to do what is right, and it must be right to curse his mother, because she spurned the right by killing the most excellent man in all the earth (811 *aristos*). So Hyllus departs, with the sarcastic wish that Deianeira may have the same joy as she bestowed on his father. He too has got it all wrong, and he will later bitterly regret his curse. That next stage is already prepared by the silent, but not unnoticed, departure of Deianeira into the house before Hyllus leaves the stage. For similar ominous exits see pp. 34 and 49.

The Chorus in its song is the first to understand the fulfilment of the old prophecy: Heracles' labours will now end, because he will be dead. We are reminded that he is the son of Zeus himself. The Chorus finds it difficult to apportion the responsibility. It was Deianeira who tried to solve the problem of Heracles' proposed marriage, but it was Nessus who ensured that her solution would be so disastrous, and the Hydra who supplied the poison. And finally it is Aphrodite, goddess of love, who has been 'clearly revealed as the doer of these deeds' (860-1).

Cries of lamentation are heard from inside the house. Enter the Nurse to report that Deianeira has killed herself by the sword, an unusual form of suicide for a woman in Greek tragedy; hanging is more normal. Deianeira's heroic 'male' death will contrast with the dying Heracles who weeps like a woman (1070-5). The Nurse narrates how, when Deianeira saw Hyllus preparing a litter for Heracles, she rushed to make up her marriage-bed. But the only bed that Heracles now requires is a litter, and he, whose homecoming has been so eagerly awaited, will never enter his house. It is on the marriage-bed that Deianeira sits to kill herself, having first said goodbye to it, the symbol of her ruined marriage. Hyllus, having learnt too late from the servants of Deianeira's good intentions, blames himself for her death. He has lost both his father and his mother.

After a song of lamentation from the Chorus, as it waits for the last time for the arrival of Heracles, the hero, probably played by the same actor as Deianeira, finally enters, carried on a litter, with an old man and attendants. Hyllus enters from the house. Heracles is still alive, at first asleep, but then in agony as he wakes up and feels the poison destroying him. The whole of this final scene presents extreme physical suffering in a way that is paralleled, among Sophocles' surviving plays, only in *Philoctetes*. Why, Heracles wonders, has Zeus rewarded him in this way for his sacrifices, and what hope is there of Zeus coming to save him? Hyllus agrees that Zeus is responsible for his father's anguish (1022). Heracles now turns his wrath against Deianeira, Hyllus' 'godless mother', and longs to see her fall, even as she has destroyed him. Of all his labours Deianeira is responsible for the worst.

Sophocles presents Heracles as callous and self-centred, and Winnington-Ingram writes that 'it might be admitted that he is one of the most unpleasant characters in Greek tragedy'. The structure of this play has, however, determined that we see him only in his suffering, and can appreciate his heroic status only through the eyes of the other characters earlier in the play, and through his own account in this final scene of his heroic exploits and benefactions.

Heracles himself points out the irony: he, the great hero, has been destroyed, not on the battlefield, nor by any of the opponents of his labours, but by a woman and without a sword. He himself in his weeping has become a woman (1070-5).

Heracles begs Hyllus to bring Deianeira so that he can kill her, and thus punish the wicked in death as he had done in life. It takes some time before Hyllus manages to convince his father that his anger is misplaced, that Deianeira 'erred unwittingly' (1123), and 'she erred through aiming to do good' (1136). It was Nessus' fault. At last Heracles understands the oracles, which now include a prophecy that he would be killed by someone already dead. This turns out to be Nessus, and the oracles which seemed to predict for him a happy life meant instead his death, since the dead have no more troubles.

Heracles wants Hyllus to burn him alive on Mount Oeta, but his shocked son demurs, and agrees only to carry him there and to arrange his funeral pyre. Heracles says that Hyllus must also marry Iole. He is not thinking of his son's welfare, but evidently sees him merely as an extension of himself. Hyllus is reluctant to do so, as Iole shares the responsibility for his mother's death and his father's suffering. As always, Hyllus wants to do what is pious and right, but Heracles persuades him that it cannot be impious or wrong to please his father. As the play ends the only joy for Heracles will be the release from his agony through death. Hyllus and Iole will marry. According to the myth they will found the famous line of the Heracleidae, 'the sons of Heracles'. But Sophocles says nothing about this. He leaves us to speculate on their chances of married bliss.

Who is responsible for all this suffering? At some point Nessus, the Hydra, Lichas, Deianeira, and Hyllus are all blamed by somebody. We may be inclined to blame also the Messenger. If he had not told Deianeira the truth about Iole, perhaps she would never have devised her plan. There is at the same time an undercurrent of criticism of the gods, most obviously of Aphrodite, whose power no person can resist, but also of Zeus himself, Heracles' father, who has done nothing to prevent his own son's suffering. On this theme the play ends, in words delivered probably by Hyllus. The final line runs, 'there is nothing in this that is not Zeus'.

As the funeral procession leaves for Oeta, the original audience perhaps derived some comfort from its knowledge that Heracles after his death would turn into a god, worshipped on Oeta with a cult. On this important point critics are divided. In the play itself there is no more than a hint of apotheosis at 1270, 'no one can foresee the future'. All the emphasis is on the suffering, on the blindness and errors of the human characters, and on the indifference of the gods. Sophocles does not attempt to explain why these things happen. How could he? This is simply the way things are.

Antigone

After the death of Oedipus, king of Thebes, his sons Eteocles and Polyneices disputed the throne. Polyneices brought an army from Argos to attack Thebes in the hope of displacing his brother, but the two of them kill each other in single combat. The play opens on the morning after the battle. Creon, the brother of Oedipus' wife Jocasta, has become king, and he immediately issues an edict stating that Eteocles is to be given an honourable funeral, but that Polyneices, as a traitor, is to be left unburied on the ground: anyone who disobeys him will be stoned to death. In the opening scene of the play we meet Antigone and Ismene, the sisters of the two brothers. Antigone, against Ismene's advice, announces her intention of disobeying the edict. She goes ahead and is eventually caught, and shut up by her uncle alone in a rock-cut tomb, where she hangs herself.

Is Antigone right or wrong to bury her brother, Creon to forbid the burial? Some critics have accepted the compromise of the nineteenth-century philosopher Hegel, who held that there is right and wrong on both sides. After the Chorus of Theban elders in its entrance-song has rejoiced over the Theban victory, in a mood of optimism that contrasts with what is to follow, Creon enters to announce the rational principles by which he intends to rule. An Athenian audience would find much of which to approve in these. Indeed, part of the speech was quoted by the fourth-century orator Demosthenes as a model of good statesmanship. But already the audience may feel that Creon is unpleasantly obsessed with his own status and position as the new king, while his rejection of the universal right to a funeral is worrying (see p. 18). At Athens in the fifth century exceptions in the case of public enemies were not unknown, and traitors too could be denied burial at home in Attica. Their bodies, however, could be thrown across the border into a neighbouring state and buried there. Creon's treatment of Polyneices must have caused at least some unease among the audience. The Chorus is less than enthusiastic in response to his announcement of his edict.

As *Antigone* progresses, the question of right and wrong becomes more and more clear-cut, as Creon begins to reveal the characteristics of the typical tyrant. It is significant that he expects opposition, and attributes the basest of material motives to those who may defy him. He sees his citizens as slaves who are to be broken in like horses (477-9). He threatens with torture and death the terrified Guard who reports that the corpse has been buried by someone unknown. The same Guard who brings Antigone under arrest to Creon, though glad to have saved his own skin by catching the culprit, shows some sympathy towards her (436-40). Creon jumps to the false conclusion that Ismene is equally responsible for the burial, and condemns her too to death. Haemon, Creon's son, who is engaged to be married to Antigone, tells him that he is wrong, that the man in the street is on Antigone's side, and tries ineffectually to persuade him to change his mind. Eventually the blind prophet Teiresias reports that the gods have already shown their anger by rejecting his sacrifices, and delivers a chilling prophecy that, because Creon has buried the living and denied burial to the dead, he will be punished by the death of his own child.

When Creon finally yields and goes off to bury Polyneices and to release Antigone from her tomb, he discovers that he has left it too late. Haemon has committed suicide beside Antigone's corpse. Creon's wife Eurydice, having heard the news, leaves the stage silently, like Deianeira in *Women of Trachis* and Jocasta in *Oedipus the King*, in order to kill herself, like Deianeira with a sword. Creon is left a broken man, himself fully admitting that he was wrong (1317-25).

When all seems so clear, one may wonder why it has ever been a matter for debate. One reason, perhaps, has been a failure to distinguish between the rightness of a person's actions, and the attractiveness, or otherwise, of that person's character. There is indeed much to dislike in Antigone. When Ismene promises to keep secret her sister's intention, Antigone replies, 'Oh no, denounce it; you will be much more my enemy if you keep silent, if you do not proclaim it to the whole world' (86-7). 'Permit me and my folly to suffer this terrible fate; for I shall suffer nothing so great as to rob me of a noble death' (95-7). It may be that for Antigone Polyneices' honour will not be restored unless his burial is publicly witnessed. But one is left with an uneasy feeling that she wants a martyr's death. This may be one reason for the double burial. The first time Antigone fulfils the required ritual by sprinkling dust on her brother's corpse. It should make no difference that Creon orders the dust to be removed. But Antigone goes back to repeat the symbolic burial. It is almost as if she wants to be caught, so that she may receive the glory for her action. In the first line of the play she addresses Ismene in terms which suggest the closest of unions between the sisters. But already by the end of the prologue she is treating Ismene as an enemy. Ismene is certainly the more attractive, and the more human, of the two. If Antigone had been more like her sister, four deaths would have been avoided. Ismene, the conventional woman, is too weak to follow her in her defiance of the king's power. Later, after Antigone has been arrested and confronts Creon, Ismene plucks up courage and tries to share with her sister the responsibility for the deed. 'How can I desire life if I am abandoned by you?' she asks (548), but Antigone scornfully replies, 'Ask Creon; for he is the one you care for.' The unfortunate Ismene, caught between Creon and Antigone, is rejected by both. Antigone does what is right, but we do not have to like her.

Antigone might appeal more obviously to a modern audience if there were greater emphasis in the play on romantic love. She never mentions Haemon, to whom, as we learn only from Ismene (568, 572), she is betrothed, and the two never meet on stage. It is true that the Chorus devotes its song at 781-800 to the theme of Eros. But, as in *Women of Trachis* (pp. 25-6), it is the destructive power of love that is stressed, and the ode is already preparing us for its effect on Haemon as much as on Antigone. Still, it would be wrong to suppose that she will abandon her fiancé easily. When she is on her way to her death she is already singing her own dirge, as one who is about to marry Death (or Acheron). Antigone and Haemon will after all be united, but only in the Underworld. Their marriage-rites will be achieved when the two corpses lie together in each other's arms. Haemon, then, provides the link between the tragedies of Antigone and Creon.

For a fifth-century Athenian audience, which may or may not have included women, the position is more complicated. Athenian society was, by modern standards, deeply chauvinistic. Except on special occasions women were expected to stay at home, and certainly they had no part to play in the political life of the city. Moreover, obedience to the laws was a matter of supreme impor-tance in a fifth-century *polis* (city-state), not least one with a democratic constitution like Athens. For at least two reasons, therefore, the original audience would look askance at Antigone, a woman who interferes in matters which are the men's concern, and who defies the laws of the city. There is perhaps a third reason. A woman was expected to marry, and when she did so, she left her father and her natal family and came under the authority of her husband. Some have thought that, by rejecting marriage in favour of her brother and her natal family, Antigone is refusing to make the conventional transition, and not behaving as a woman should. The paradox is that the character who starts off with all these disadvantages is the one who makes the right decision.

Some critics have held that, while in the eyes of the gods Creon was wrong to leave the corpse unburied, Antigone, as a woman, was wrong to bury it. Certainly the gods will not reward her for her action (see p. 39); they will leave her to her fate. But it is wrong to conclude from this that the gods think that she deserves her pun-ishment. When no male relative is available, or willing, to do what is right, the woman is morally obliged to do it. 'Antigone's moral difference in the end serves to raise questions about, and expose contradictions in, Creon's mode of morality, and hence indirectly to problematize, as tragedy often does, Athenian civic values and discourse' (Foley).

As with *Women of Trachis* (p. 21), scholars have disagreed as to which is the principal character of the play. On the one hand, Creon has by far the larger number of spoken lines, and only he is, except for the prologue, on stage in every scene of the play. Antigone disappears some two-thirds of the way through the play, and she is hardly mentioned by Creon in the final scene. The bodies of Haemon and Eurydice will be brought on to the stage, but not Antigone's.

On the other hand, the play is called *Antigone*, and everything in it springs from her refusal to obey Creon's edict. More important, it is she who behaves like the hero whom we recognise from other Sophoclean plays, the person who is resolute in doing what he or she believes to be right, who refuses to listen to the common-sense advice of the minor characters, or to learn moderation or restraint (*sophrosyne*). Antigone never changes her mind, but Creon does. He refuses, indeed, to listen to Haemon, who, in the kind of language found in other Sophoclean plays (715-18), begs him to yield. But then he reprieves Ismene, and betrays his uneasiness by announcing that, instead of stoning Antigone (cf. p. 33), he will shut her up in the rock-cut tomb: she will die 'naturally' of starvation. After the intervention of the seer Teiresias he finally agrees to yield (1096-9), an extraordinary change of mind for a Sophoclean hero, and goes off to bury Polyneices and to release Antigone from her tomb. Creon's problem is that, while he has at last decided to do the right thing, he has left the decision too late. Even now, if he had gone first to the tomb, he might have arrived before Antigone had time to commit suicide. In the final scene Creon, as he acknowledges his error, is led away a broken man. Contrast the dignity of Oedipus at the end of *Oedipus the King*, or of Ajax in his final suicide-speech. It is Antigone, not Creon, who behaves as we expect a Sophoclean hero to behave.

The attempt to distinguish a single principal character is

probably doomed to failure (see p. 21). In this play it is the interaction between *two* characters that leads to tragedy for them both. This does not entirely eliminate the problem of Antigone's disappearance so early in the play, and one can understand why for some critics this is another 'diptych'-play (pp. 16 and 21). In *Ajax* we could at least see the corpse of Ajax while the wrangling proceeded over the question of its burial. But, if this is a defect in the structure of the play, it should not be exaggerated. In the final scenes, although our attention is concentrated on Creon, we do not forget Antigone. It is Creon's repentance that indirectly proves that Antigone was right, in the eyes of gods as well as men, to bury her brother, just as in *Ajax* it was the final decision to allow the burial that vindicated Ajax's heroic status.

For both characters, then, the outcome is tragic, but in very different ways. Creon's tragedy is that of a sincere but misguided man, who, confident in his own intellectual powers of reasoning, accuses Antigone of folly, but learns in the end that he himself is the fool. Proud of his rationality, he reveals his irrational prejudices against women, young men like Haemon, and any citizen who may oppose him, and in his lyric lamentation at the end he is emotionally shattered. He thinks that he is acting in the interests of the *polis*, but brings pollution upon it. His rejection of family ties results in the deaths of his own son and his wife. Eurydice, who is hardly a character in her own right, is brought in merely to deepen Creon's suffering. He has lost his entire family. His sententious and rhetorically constructed speeches reveal his intellectual pride. 'I know', he says repeatedly. Sophocles' famous irony is sometimes verbal, but often it is deeper. It marks the gap between appearances, what the characters believe, and the reality of which only the audience is aware. So here, the man who prides himself on his knowledge turns out to be the man who knows nothing.

Antigone shows much less concern for rational arguments. For her it is all a matter of feeling. As early as the opening scene with Ismene she makes it clear that she will bury Polyneices simply because he is her brother and Creon has no right to keep her from doing so. That the gods demand a proper funeral for all corpses is an argument merely hinted at (77), and will be used by Antigone only in the confrontation-scene with Creon (450-60), when, forced to give some kind of rational excuse for her action, she argues that the unwritten divine laws must take precedence over human edicts. But by the end of that speech she has returned to her feelings: it would have pained her to leave her brother unburied on the ground (466-8). In her final speech she says that it was only because Polyneices was her brother that she buried him. If he had been her husband or her child, she would not have bothered; for these would have been replaceable. Critics have been puzzled by the frigid calculation that her words imply, and some have even thought that this part of the speech must be a later interpolation in the text, modelled perhaps on a story in Herodotus. Rather, we should see the speech as a final desperate attempt to justify her action logically. It does not succeed because in this area Antigone is out of her depth. What is more important is that she remains confident to the end that she was right. Some critics have found a moment of self-doubt when, at the end of her speech (925-6), she says that if the gods approve of her death she will learn after she has suffered it that she was wrong. But the tone is rather one of indignation, and all the emphasis is on the following clause, 'but if they [my enemies] are wrong ...'. Antigone's tragedy is that she suffers for doing what is right.

Moreover Sophocles has taken care to show us that, although she is right, she, like other Sophoclean heroes, is isolated in her suffering. Usually in Greek tragedy a heroine is supported by a female chorus. Here the Chorus of male elders, while it shows some sympathy, is more disposed to criticise Antigone. Earlier she had envisaged a heroic martyr's death by public stoning. What she now faces is quite a different matter. She goes to it without ever hearing Haemon's report of public opinion, and she does not understand why the gods have let her down (922-4). Sophocles does not explain why the gods let her suffer for doing what is right. What answer could there be? It is this that makes Antigone's tragedy deeper than Creon's.

The play presents not so much a clash of principles as a conflict between two people, each of whom is incapable of understanding the other's point of view. As Mary Blundell has shown most thoroughly, the theme of friends and enemies provides the key to the understanding of the play. These English words are inadequate to translate the Greek *philoi* and *echthroi*. The former, for a Greek audience, include not only friends but also one's family, one's nearest and dearest, all those with whom one enjoys a positive relationship, while the rest of the world may be expected to be hostile. It was a cardinal principle of Greek ethics that one should do good to one's friends, and harm to one's enemies. We have met it already in *Ajax*. But the potential for conflict arises when loyalties clash, when the categories become confused.

The opening scene makes it clear that relationships are going to be all-important, when Antigone tells Ismene that 'the troubles of enemies are coming on friends' (10). The language is enigmatic, but she seems to mean that her brother Polyneices, who as a member of the family, ought to be a friend, is being treated by Creon as an enemy (or perhaps, that her enemies [Creon] are bringing trouble on her friends [Polyneices]). The play begins with Antigone claiming to be a friend of her sister, but already by the end of the prologue she is treating her as an enemy. Ismene, on the other hand, declares (99), according to the best interpretation, that she will always be her friend. For Creon it is all a matter of politics; the only true friend is the friend of the city (182-91). Polyneices is a traitor, so he cannot be his friend. The conflict comes to a head when Antigone and Creon, members of the same family but now enemies, confront each other in brisk, line-by-line dialogue (508-25). Antigone, with no interest in political friendship, says that Polyneices died not as Eteocles' slave but as his brother, while Creon declares, 'an enemy will never be a friend, even when he is dead'. Antigone replies, 'my nature is not to join in hating, but to join in loving'. Again the words are enigmatic, but the tangle of relationships is clear. Creon's final words are, 'well, go do down below, and love them if love you must; as long as I live, no woman will rule over me'.

With such a gulf between them tragedy is inevitable for them both. It is sometimes said that they should have looked for a compromise, but in such a conflict compromise would be impossible. Either it was right or it was wrong for Antigone to bury Polyneices; there was no middle road. The double burial allows Sophocles to have the Chorus sing a famous song at 332-75. It has heard that someone has sprinkled dust on the corpse, but does not yet know who the culprit is. In its uncertainty it celebrates the supreme achievements of the human intellect, the intellect on which Creon has prided himself. But at the end there is a moment of doubt: there is, as well as the technological, a moral sphere, in which human ingenuity has not always been so successful. Cleverness can lead to disaster.

The theme of the ode at 781-800 (pp. 35-6) is the *irrational* power of love. And at 1115-54 it is the equally irrational Dionysus whom the Chorus celebrates, in the mistaken belief that everything is going to end happily. It is the emotional, irrational Antigone, not the intellectual, rational Creon, who turns out to be right. Human wisdom is not necessarily the answer to our problems.

Oedipus the King

Oedipus the King is perhaps the most celebrated of all Sophocles' plays. It was also evidently the favourite of the fourth-century philosopher Aristotle, for whom in his *Poetics* it illustrates perfectly his theory of the best kind of tragedy, one which presents someone of high reputation and prosperity who falls into misfortune, not because he is wicked, but because of some mistake. At the beginning of the play he is at the height of his powers as king of Thebes, the father of his people, the good king to whom it naturally turns when afflicted by plague and sterility. Though not equal to the gods (it would be blasphemous to call him that), he is regarded as the first and the best of men (33, 46), the saviour who once before had rescued the city from the ravages of the monstrous Sphinx (48). By the end of the play he has discovered that he has committed the most terrible crimes of killing his own father and marrying his own mother, and that he himself, through his unnatural procreation of children by his mother, is responsible for the plague and sterility in the land.

Before Oedipus was born, Laius, king of Thebes, received an oracle from Apollo at Delphi, which said that he would have a son who would kill him and marry his mother Jocasta. To prevent the fulfilment of the prophecy, Laius and Jocasta arranged for their new-born baby to be exposed on Mount Cithaeron. However, the servant entrusted with the task handed him over to a shepherd from Corinth, who took him home and presented him to the king and queen of Corinth, Polybus and Merope, who brought him up as their own son. When he grew up, taunted with illegitimacy by a drunken man at a party, he went to Delphi to enquire about the truth of his birth. But the oracle told him only that he would kill his father and marry his mother. Thinking that they were Polybus and Merope, he resolved never to return to Corinth. Instead he turned towards Thebes, but on the way, at a place where three roads met (i.e. where the road forked) he encountered an old man with his retinue, and in a brawl he killed them all, except for one servant who escaped. The unrecognised old man was his father Laius, on his way to Delphi to consult the oracle. Oedipus proceeded to Thebes, where he killed the Sphinx by solving her riddle (What goes on four feet, two feet, and three feet? The answer is 'man'), and received from the grateful Thebans the throne of Laius and his own mother in marriage.

All of this happened before the play begins. The subject of the play itself is not Oedipus' crimes, but his discovery that he has committed them, and his reaction to that discovery. Much of its appeal for modern readers may derive from its resemblance in some respects to a detective-novel. When, early in the play, Jocasta's brother Creon returns from Delphi to report Apollo's oracle that the city will be saved if the pollution can be driven out, Oedipus, so proud of his intellectual powers, is confident of his ability to find the killer of Laius, as his cleverness in solving the riddle has already saved the city from the Sphinx. But he does not know that the polluted person, and the one responsible for the plague, is himself. When, therefore, he issues his public proclamation against the 'unknown' killer(s), it is his own fate that he is sealing.

In this play Sophoclean irony is more prominent than in any other. It becomes almost overpowering in Oedipus' speech at 132-46 as he begins his investigation: 'it is not on behalf of distant friends [he means Laius] but on my own behalf that I shall eliminate this pollution … in helping him I help myself'. The irony is more than verbal (cf. p. 38). It springs from Sophocles' deep conviction that human beings by their very nature are flawed and incapable of full understanding. The gap between seeming and reality is no-where clearer than here, where the man who thinks that he knows, or can find out, everything, is in fact ignorant even of his own identity. Only Teiresias, with his divine insight, and the play's audience know the truth. The audience is, as it were, in the position of the gods themselves. While we identify largely with the characters, Sophoclean irony requires also that we remain to some extent detached.

We might expect that the truth will only gradually be revealed to Oedipus. Perhaps he will find out first that he was the killer of Laius, and then the further revelation will follow that Laius was his father and Jocasta his mother. But this is not what happens. By a daring dramatic stroke Sophocles has the prophet Teiresias reveal the truth quite early in the play. Having been sent for by Oedipus to help with his investigation into the killer of Laius, Teiresias arrives determined to say nothing. Oedipus, then, is ignorant but determined to know, whereas Teiresias knows the truth but is determined to suppress it. He is the first of three persons in the play who will attempt to stop Oedipus from going on with his investigation. Note again the irony: Teiresias is physically blind (the Chorus-leader draws attention to the paradox at 284-6), while Oedipus, the physically sighted, knows nothing. Late in the play, when at last he discovers the truth, he will blind himself, in his horror unable to face the world, and will thus be in the position of Teiresias here. Teiresias' refusal to help him save the city naturally angers Oedipus, whose taunts then have the effect of enraging the prophet, so that before the scene ends he who was resolved to say nothing about the killer of Laius not only reveals (362) that it was Oedipus himself but also gratuitously adds a strong hint of the latter's true parentage: 'He will turn out to be living with his own children as alike their brother and their father, both the son and husband of the woman who gave him birth, who sowed seed in the bed of, and who killed, his father' (457-60). Oedipus has been told the truth but he refuses to believe it. Human blindness could hardly be displayed more strongly.

Sophocles' dramatic strategy will succeed only if he can convince us that Oedipus' inability to grasp the truth is reasonable, given his character and the circumstances in which the truth is revealed to him. He is, after all, supposed to be a clever intellectual, and we know that he solved the riddle of the Sphinx. From very early on Sophocles makes it clear that his failure is almost inevitable. When Creon tells him about the killing of Laius, Oedipus asks if there was no eyewitness. Creon's reply is crucial: 'They [i.e. Laius' retinue] all died, except for some one man, who fled in fear, and he was unable to tell with knowledge anything of what he saw except one thing' (118-19). Oedipus seizes upon this one clue, seeing it as the key to the discovery of the truth. But the one thing that the servant was able to reveal was that Laius had been murdered, not by an individual, but by a large band of robbers. Out of shame at his failure to defend his master he had doubtless suppressed the truth. So from the very beginning the investigation has got off to a false start; all of Oedipus' confidence is based upon a lie. Totally unaware of the crucial distinction between singular and plural, he goes on to surmise that the 'robber' (singular – Segal calls it 'a kind of Freudian slip of the tongue') must have been bribed by political conspirators.

In the quarrel-scene with Teiresias this false, but entirely reasonable, suspicion of an attempted political coup becomes the second obstacle to Oedipus' discovery of the truth. His anger may remind us uncomfortably of that which he had displayed when he killed Laius, but it is also the natural response to Teiresias' refusal to co-operate. Teiresias' only possible motive, it seems to Oedipus, is that he was an accomplice in the conspiracy. Since, however, being blind he could not carry it out himself, the suspicion must point to Creon, who was next in line to the throne. It was Creon too who had suggested the consultation with Teiresias (288; cf. 555-6). Why, in any case, should Oedipus believe the prophecies of Teiresias (390-400)? It was Oedipus, not Teiresias, who in his wisdom had solved the riddle of the Sphinx. We can understand why he jumps to all the wrong conclusions. The irony, however, is that this natural anger is preventing him from grasping the truth. In the ode that follows the Chorus refuses to condemn its king; prophets, after all, can be wrong. Everyone, except for Teiresias, is still trapped in the world of delusion.

In the following episode Oedipus confronts Creon with his suspicions, and finally condemns him to death. The quarrel in a sense parallels the earlier one with Teiresias, but there is an important difference. Unlike Teiresias, Creon, a model of *sophrosyne*, does not lose his temper with his brother-in-law, but argues calmly and reasonably that he has no ambitious desire for the throne. As so often in Sophocles, it is the minor characters whose behaviour is more attractive than the hero's. Oedipus, the good king, is not a tyrant, but he is acting more and more as if he were. Yet it is Oedipus, with his relentless search for the truth, whom we admire. Creon is a little too complacent. He is unwilling to accept the responsibilities of kingship, but Oedipus knows that he himself 'must rule' (628).

Jocasta now makes her first appearance from the palace. She has come to learn what all the noise is about. She succeeds in calming the quarrel, and the reluctant Oedipus is persuaded by the Chorus to repeal his death-sentence against Creon. His death would serve no dramatic purpose in the play. To reassure her husband that there is no need to believe *human* prophets such as Teiresias, she narrates, for the first time in the play, the story of the oracle given to Laius (but omitting the prophecy that his son will marry his mother), and of the killing at the place where three roads meet. Laius was killed not by his son but by robbers, so the oracle, as presented by its human interpreters, was wrong. However, instead of reassuring Oedipus, by mentioning the scene of Laius' killing she merely increases his anxiety. Unintentionally Jocasta has initiated the move from the world of appearance to that of reality.

Oedipus explains his worry by narrating his visit to Delphi, and his killing of an elderly stranger at the place where three roads meet. He includes also the prophecy that he will marry his mother and kill his father, but as yet he has no suspicion of his true parentage. His fear now is that he may after all be the killer of Laius, and that, if so, he has cursed himself. At last the significance of the number of robbers becomes clear to him. The servant, already summoned at 765, must be fetched as quickly as possible from the countryside where he now lives. There is still room for hope. If he confirms that there was a plurality of robbers, Oedipus will be set free from his growing anxiety. Jocasta, in reassurance, adds that, even if he changes his story, Apollo (she no longer distinguishes the god from his human interpreters) was wrong to tell Laius that he would be killed by his son.

After a difficult but important ode from the troubled Chorus (see p. 51), Sophocles presents one of his most startling dramatic strokes. The Chorus has ended its song by deploring the decline in religious belief (909-10), but now a worried Jocasta appears, her scepticism forgotten, engaged in the practices of conventional religion, on her way to offer sacrifices and praying to Apollo for help. Religion is not perishing after all. Immediately, however, a man dressed in country clothes appears. He enters by a side-passage from the country. We learned at 757-64 from Jocasta that the servant who had witnessed Laius' killing had asked to be sent away from the palace to the countryside. Sophocles was already preparing us for the present moment. If the servant had still been living in the palace he would have had to emerge through the central door. As it is, the audience, already expecting him to enter by the side-passage from the country, naturally assumes that here is the long awaited eyewitness, and that he will immediately be questioned about the number of the killers. Oedipus will learn that he is indeed the killer of Laius, and Sophocles will then turn to the revelation of his parentage. But that is not what happens. The countryman turns out, quite unexpectedly, to be a messenger from Corinth, with the news that Polybus is dead and Oedipus has succeeded to the throne. Jocasta and, on his arrival, Oedipus are naturally delighted. The latter's 'father' has died naturally, and Oedipus is freed from the fear of killing him. Apollo's oracle has proved to be false, not just its human interpreters, and Jocasta's pious exercise of conventional religion has turned out to be unnecessary.

However, Oedipus is still troubled by the fear that he may marry his mother. To reassure him the Messenger reveals that he is not the son of Polybus and Merope, and explains how he himself had received the baby from a Theban shepherd. But his attempt at reassurance has the opposite effect on Jocasta, just as earlier her own attempt at reassuring Oedipus had had the opposite effect on him (see p. 47). Jocasta immediately grasps the truth, and at the end of the episode departs, silently like Deianeira and Eurydice (pp. 28 and 34), to commit suicide inside the palace. Before she goes, she, like Teiresias earlier (p. 45), tries unsuccessfully to stop Oedipus from seeking to learn more. But Oedipus is completely preoccupied now with discovering the secret of his birth. His excitement contrasts with her horror, which itself contrasts with the joyous mood with which the episode began. This new preoccupation is the final obstacle to Oedipus' search for the killer of Laius. That search has turned into the search for his own identity. Laius is forgotten, as is his earlier determination to save the city from the plague.

The Chorus, caught up in Oedipus' excitement and sharing in his final delusion, speculates in a happy ode about his possible parentage. As in other plays (pp. 15 and 41), the cheerful mood comes immediately before the horror, and makes the final revelation all the darker. The Theban Shepherd, summoned for interrogation about the killing of Laius, arrives knowing only that the killer is Oedipus. Now he confronts the Messenger, who knows only that Oedipus is the baby who should have died on Cithaeron. It is the combination of their knowledge that reveals everything to Oedipus. The Theban Shepherd, who is the first to grasp the truth, is the third character to urge Oedipus to abandon his investigation. But Oedipus, as always, is determined to know. The two servants depart, and the Theban Shepherd has never been interrogated about the killing of Laius. That question has been overtaken by the much more serious revelation. The Chorus' ode on the transitory nature of all human happiness contrasts strongly with its previous song.

Perhaps the most debated problem of the play concerns the responsibility for Oedipus' fall. Many modern readers have a strong impression that everything was fated, and that it was therefore not his fault. Even before he was born the oracle predicted that Laius would have a son, who would kill his father and marry his mother. In other versions of the story the oracle said that *if* Laius had a son, that son would kill him. But in Sophocles there is no *if*. The parents thought that they could thwart the oracle by exposing the baby, but oracles cannot be frustrated, as Oedipus and Jocasta discover in the play. Oedipus, when he receives his response from the same oracle at Delphi, avoids going back to Corinth, but, by what we might call a terrible coincidence, encounters his real father at the place where three roads meet, and duly kills him. It is then through the virtuous act of saving Thebes from the Sphinx that he is rewarded with his mother in marriage. How can he be blamed for what he did in ignorance? Even the killing of the supposed stranger can be justified as an act of self-defence. Sophocles never tries to explain whether or why Apollo wanted all this to happen. The relationship between the gods and fate is inconsistently described as early as Homer. Sometimes fate seems more powerful than the gods, while at other times it is apparently identified with the will of the gods themselves. Here it is possible to argue that Apollo, being as a god omniscient, knew what would happen in the future, but did not himself plan that future. He knew that a man with a certain character, when he found himself in a certain situation, would inevitably behave in a certain way.

For other readers it is the character of Oedipus that is all-important, and it is true that he himself never denies responsibility for his actions. It is not so much his crimes as his discovery of them that leads to his fall, and the oracle did not predict that discovery or his fall. It is Oedipus himself, in his admirable desire to save his city, who begins the investigation, and who, in publicly cursing the unknown killer of Laius, inadvertently curses himself. Throughout the play he persists in his investigation, despite the three attempts by other characters to make him abandon it. When the Theban Shepherd cries, 'alas, I am on the terrible brink of speaking', Oedipus replies, 'and I of hearing; but still I must hear' (1169-70; cf. 1065). His desire to save the city and his search for the truth seem wholly admirable, and the play gives little reason to suppose that, if he had not insisted on it, fate, or Apollo, would have found some other means of bringing him down. But no Sophoclean hero is perfect, and some critics have suggested that his pride in his intellectual powers is excessive, and that the gods are punishing him for it. It is hard to reconcile this judgement with the fact that his crimes were foretold before his birth.

Others point to his hybristic behaviour towards Teiresias and Creon, which may be in the mind of the pious Chorus in its ode at 863-910, the starting point of which seems to be Jocasta's scepticism about oracles. The Chorus is worried that those who commit *hybris* may escape punishment, and that if oracles are not fulfilled religious practice and belief will decline (see p. 48). But Sophocles is not using the Chorus as his mouthpiece to condemn Oedipus (or Jocasta), or to preach a simple sermon. Nor does the Chorus seriously hope that the oracle can still be saved through the discovery that Laius was killed by his son, and so not by Oedipus – still less that Oedipus will turn out to be both killer and son; for at this stage the Chorus 'knows' that Laius has no surviving son. No one can really suppose that Oedipus falls because he loses his temper with Teiresias and Creon. Rather, Sophocles is using his Chorus to express a deeply-felt human yearning for a clear link between morality and prosperity. We would all like the wicked to be punished, and the good to prosper. If this does not happen, what is the good of religion?

In fact the oracle will turn out to have been fulfilled, and conventional piety will after all be saved, but at the cost of Oedipus' ruin. In a sense the Chorus puts the question the wrong way round. Instead of worrying about the wicked who escape punishment, it should perhaps be worrying about the innocent Oedipus who is heading for a fall. But then, if we think more deeply, is he really innocent? He did not know what he was doing, but could any of us feel free from guilt, if we discovered what Oedipus discovered? Sophocles gives no simple answers, but, by means of his Chorus, he indicates the insoluble questions which underlie his tragic conception.

It seems that both fate and Oedipus' own character are responsible for his fall. Some have argued that, while his crimes were wholly fated, he himself is entirely responsible for his investigation of the truth and for his self-blinding. However, our own experience contradicts the notion that at one stage of his life a man's actions are wholly determined by outside forces, while at another he must accept full responsibility for them. It is contradicted also by the play itself. Oedipus would never have begun his investigation had it not been for the plague, which it is not unreasonable to ascribe to Apollo, the god who causes the plague in the Greek army at Troy in Book 1 of the *Iliad*. It is a mysterious divine power that leads Oedipus to the scene of Jocasta's suicide. And, when the Chorus at 1328 asks him which of the gods caused him to blind himself, he replies, 'it was Apollo, Apollo, my friends, who brought to completion these my cruel, cruel sufferings', but then he adds, 'but my eyes were struck by no one else's hands; I did it, wretched me, myself'. Oedipus sees the whole complex of events as doubly determined, by the outside power represented by Apollo, and by his own deliberate actions. This may seem illogical, but it is consistent with our own experience. All that we do is, to a greater or less extent, predetermined by our genes, by our environment, by the pressure of circumstances or other people, and by our own earlier choices and decisions. But we are still responsible. Oedipus would not have fallen if he had not been the kind of man he was.

So far we have talked about Oedipus' fall. Yet something has been gained. We may assume that the city has been saved from its plague and infertility, though nothing is made of this at the end of the play. More important, in one sense Oedipus does not fall at all. He set out to uncover the truth, and by the end of the play he has succeeded in his quest. It is the minor characters who try to stop him. Teiresias says, 'how terrible it is to have wisdom when it brings no profit to the man who has it' (316-17), and Jocasta, 'ill-fated man, may you never learn who you are' (1068). We might be inclined to agree, but Oedipus himself does not. As the play ends Oedipus has lost his throne, he is blind, and has to say a poignant good-bye to his beloved daughters as he prepares to leave them. It is left strangely unclear whether he departs directly by a side-passage to his exile (which is what he wants), or, as is more probable (see Taplin), into the now hated palace to wait upon the advice of Apollo (as Creon, correct but cold to the end, decrees at 1438-43). To the original audience the staging would make it clear. Oedipus seems to have lost everything, and of course he is devastated by the discovery of what he has done. But he never says, 'I wish I had not found out'; for he has gained what he values most – knowledge no matter what it costs. He is the only character for whom to live a painless lie is worse than to accept a painful truth. So to the end of the play Oedipus remains true to himself, and it is he, not Teiresias, Creon, or Jocasta, whom we admire. Pessimism and optimism, as so often in Sophocles, are combined at the end of the play.

Electra

On his return home from the Trojan War Agamemnon was murdered by his wife Clytaemnestra and her lover Aegisthus. Orestes,
Agamemnon's son, comes home from exile, is recognised by his
sister Electra, and takes vengeance on his father's murderers. The
story, already alluded to in Homer's *Odyssey*, was the subject of
Aeschylus' *Libation Bearers*, produced in 458 BC. It was treated
also by Euripides in his *Electra*. The dates of Sophocles' and
Euripides' plays are unfortunately unknown, so that, while it is
clear that they were both influenced by Aeschylus' version, it is
impossible to know for sure which of the two younger playwrights
had the other's play in front of him. Since, however, Euripides'
version represents the more radical departure from the traditional
story, one may argue that it was the last of the three to be composed.

In *Libation Bearers* the main action focuses on Orestes' vengeance,
and Electra disappears from the stage before that vengeance takes
place. But both Sophocles and Euripides shift the focus, as the titles
of their plays indicate, to Electra. Whereas in Aeschylus the
recognition-scene between Orestes and Electra occurs early in the
play, and in Euripides comparatively early, the most notable feature
of Sophocles' play-construction is that it comes almost at the end,
and is given an unusually full treatment, while the actual killing of
Clytaemnestra and Aegisthus is handled very briefly, and almost
perfunctorily, in the final scene. If we can find the answer as to why
Sophocles has arranged matters in this way, we may have found
also the key to understanding his whole dramatic concept.

It may be helpful to work backwards from the recognition-scene
to the beginning of the play, as Sophocles may conceivably have
done himself as he planned its construction. The recognition cannot

come until Electra, in a scene climactic for her emergence as a Sophoclean hero, has made her great decision to kill the murderers herself. But that scene has to follow the false news brought by the old Paedagogus (the servant who had looked after Orestes as a child) that her beloved brother Orestes is dead. Until now she has depended on Orestes to carry out the vengeance, but now she knows that she is alone, and will have to do the job herself. If, however, we are to understand the effect of the 'Messenger-scene' on Electra, Sophocles must first present to us her emotional state when she still hopes that her brother will return. Every scene is in exactly the right place, and the structure of the play seems almost inevitable.

We have not yet, however, gone back quite to the beginning. First we meet Orestes and the Paedagogus, who has brought him up for this moment when he can at last take vengeance on his father's murderers. Orestes is accompanied by his faithful friend Pylades, who has no speaking part in this play. The plan is made. Apollo's oracle has told him to use deceit. The Paedagogus, therefore, will come to the palace with the news that Orestes has been killed in a chariot-race at the Pythian Games at Delphi, and then Orestes himself will appear carrying an urn which will be supposed to contain his ashes. The time for action has come, and there is a strong sense of urgency. Orestes looks forward to the glory that his deed will bring him. It will be his first act of manhood, and his role in the play has been compared to the rite of passage which young Athenian males underwent as *ephebes* in their transition from adolescence to adult maturity (cf. p. 68). Orestes is emotionally detached. He expresses no scruples at the thought that he is about to kill his mother, and the audience is not encouraged to think about the horror of the deed. The tone as a whole is brisk and business-like. There is a job to be done, and we look forward to the fulfilment of the plan. But we will be kept waiting for that fulfilment until the very end of the play. The preparation and the fulfilment provide the framework of the play. All that happens in between concerns Electra rather than Orestes.

Suddenly the mood changes. Electra's voice is heard from inside the palace, and it is significant that it is a cry of lamentation. The unemotional Orestes is about to be replaced on stage by his highly emotional sister. Orestes (if we may trust the distribution of the lines in the manuscripts) thinks that it may be his sister's voice – already he is unconsciously drawn towards her. But the Paedagogus hurries him away so that they can make offerings at Agamemnon's tomb, thereby frustrating the recognition-scene which for a moment we expect. Electra appears, and, in an anapaestic soliloquy, reveals to the audience the two themes which dominate her existence, the one in the past, the other in the future – her father's murder, which she will lament for ever, and her longing for her brother to return and take vengeance on behalf of them both. Orestes' return and her desire for vengeance are inseparable in Electra's mind. For the audience the irony is that Orestes *has* returned, and is already planning the vengeance.

The Chorus of women of Mycenae enters, and joins Electra in an emotional lyric song. Though sympathetic to her plight, it urges her to restrain her lamentation, to learn moderation, as excess will bring her only further trouble. The attempt by a chorus, or a minor character, to teach the hero sense and moderation, we have already met in Sophocles' earlier plays. Electra's feeling of isolation and her refusal to listen or to compromise are equally typical of the Sophoclean hero. If she were to take the Chorus' advice she feels that she would no longer be true to herself, and we admire her for her single-mindedness. Yet, unlike Orestes in the prologue, she is herself aware that there is something unnatural about her behaviour: 'In a terrible situation I have come under a terrible compulsion – I know, I am aware of my temper' (221-2). She picks up the same theme in her iambic speech to the Chorus at 254-7, when she says that she is ashamed of her excessive lamentation, but she has been forced into it (cf. 309). So she will continue to lament and to long for her brother's return. The trouble is that he never comes (168-72; cf. 303-6, 319). For the present she can annoy the usurpers by her behaviour and her words, so that for Electra words *are* a form of action, but, until Orestes returns, there is nothing that she can do that will really avenge her father's death in the way that matters.

Enter Chrysothemis, Electra's sister, carrying offerings. She has come to make a further attack on Electra's resolution. In many ways she plays the same role as Ismene in *Antigone*. While accepting that Electra is right (338-9, an important admission for guiding the sympathy of the audience), she explains that she is too weak to follow her, and prefers a comfortable life. Her sister, she reports, is to be imprisoned because of her behaviour. Electra, she argues, would do well to follow her own path of compromise, to yield to those who are stronger than she is (396), and to learn common sense and moderation. Like Antigone, Electra refuses to take the advice. Her idea of a good life is very different from that of her sister (392-5). There is not yet, however, a complete breakdown in the sisters' relationship. Chrysothemis explains that she is on her way to Agamemnon's tomb, with propitiatory offerings from Clytaemnestra. The latter has had a nightmare which has warned her of her husband's anger. Electra persuades her sister to hide, or throw away, the offerings, and to substitute a lock of hair from each of the girls, with the prayer that Orestes may come and triumph over her enemies. Chrysothemis agrees to do so. For the first time in the play Electra has been able to move forward from largely passive lamentation and hoping, and to take a positive practical step. If Clytaemnestra is afraid, that must mean that things are going well for Electra. It may be the spirit of the dead Agamemnon that has sent the dream from below the earth. The audience knows that, with Orestes already home, her confidence is justified. With equal confidence the Chorus, in a brief ode, looks forward to the coming of Justice (476). We are not invited to remember that Justice in this case means the murder of a mother by her son. The only disquieting notes are a reference to the avenging Fury (491; see p. 63), and a reminder of the ancient curse on the family.

So far we have seen Electra in the company only of her sympathisers. It is time now to see her resolution tested in a confrontation with her enemy, Clytaemnestra. In a long speech the latter sets out her justification for murdering her husband, and in an even longer speech Electra demolishes her arguments. The audience may feel some misgivings when even Clytaemnestra can claim to have Justice on her side (528), and Electra does not seem to think that the question is important ('whether [you killed Agamemnon] justly or not' 560). She even concedes that her own behaviour may be shameless, but claims that she has inherited it from her mother (606-9). 'Shameful deeds', she says (621), 'are taught by shameful deeds'. We might say, 'like mother, like daughter'. The audience, then, may have some nagging doubts, but on the whole it is clearly Electra who comes off better in the quarrel. Her mother deserves her punishment. Clytaemnestra prays to Apollo that her dream may turn out after all to portend good for her, that she may continue to enjoy the fruits of her crime, and that the god will grant her what she cannot express openly, meaning clearly that Orestes will die. The prayer is both blasphemous and futile. We know that Orestes is already home, brought by the very god to whom she prays.

At this moment the Paedagogus appears, as if in immediate answer to her prayer, with the news that Orestes is indeed dead. One might compare the sudden appearance of the Corinthian Messenger in *Oedipus the King* (p. 48) with news that apparently relieves Jocasta of all her fears. But the effect is quite different. There the audience shuddered at its knowledge of the true situation. Here we enjoy watching Clytaemnestra so deluded. Soon Electra will be reunited with her brother, and Clytaemnestra will get what she deserves. The immediate first reaction is that of the totally despairing Electra. Clytaemnestra asks for details of Orestes' death. The Paedagogus, in accordance with Orestes' orders in the prologue, recounts how Orestes, after winning many prizes in the Pythian Games, displayed supreme skill in the chariot-race, only to crash at the end. This is the longest formal messenger-speech in the surviving plays of Sophocles, which makes it all the more remarkable that from beginning to end it is a lie. Why is it so long? The main reason is, no doubt, that Sophocles wants to keep us waiting for Clytaemnestra's full reaction and for the development of that which really matters, the reaction of Electra. If her hope has gone, what is she going to do now? At the same time the story presents to us Orestes as a natural victor, the true son of his father, and thus foreshadows the real victory which the Paedagogus and the audience expect him to achieve. Yet it is told in such a way as to arouse a few misgivings. The spectators at the Games called Orestes blessed (693), a dangerous title for any mortal to receive, as it might attract the resentment of the gods. And then he crashed his chariot, having made an error in rounding the turning-post, the very manoeuvre at which he had seemed to be most skilful. Success, in Greek thought, is so often followed by a fall. We may think of Oedipus, who prided himself on his intellectual skill, but who turned out to know nothing. It is, of course, all a lie, but can we be completely satisfied that his real victory will be unsullied? At the very least, we are involved with Electra in her despair.

Clytaemnestra's reaction may surprise us slightly. She does not know, she says, whether to mourn her son or to rejoice. Even Clytaemnestra is not entirely black. She takes the Paedagogus into the house, and Electra remains outside with the Chorus. This is almost her darkest moment. Gone is the hope that was roused by the report of Clytaemnestra's dream. For years she has longed for the return of her brother and for vengeance. Without Orestes there can be no hope of vengeance. If Electra was isolated before, she now feels totally alone and friendless. The audience can have little idea of what will happen next, but certainly the play cannot end with Electra standing outside the palace, vowing never to enter it again.

We have probably forgotten Chrysothemis, whom we last saw departing to Agamemnon's tomb. She now makes an entrance which is as startling as that of the Paedagogus earlier (p. 59). In the last line of her lyric dialogue with the Chorus (870) Electra has complained that she was unable to lament at her brother's funeral. In her first line Chrysothemis speaks of joy; she has found Orestes' offerings at the tomb, and so he must have come home safely. If this had happened before the Paedagogus scene, it would have fed the hope inspired in Electra by Clytaemnestra's dream. But now Electra 'knows' that Orestes is dead, and her sister's joy makes her despair all the blacker. This is her lowest moment. Ironically she who is deluded pours scorn on Chrysothemis' delusion, which is in fact the truth, and she reduces her sister to her own despair.

Then, very quietly, an upward movement begins. There is something, she says, that they can do to alleviate their present trouble. Chrysothemis is eager to help, until she finds out what that something is. Electra's proposal is that they kill Aegisthus by themselves. We sense that she is glad when Chrysothemis refuses, so that the glory of her deed will be hers alone. The relationship between the sisters has turned to enmity, but for Electra it is now the moment to rise to her full stature as a Sophoclean hero. In her total isolation she rejects the advice of the 'normal' woman, Chrysothemis, and, like Antigone, finds the resolution to adopt the role of the male. She looks forward to being honoured for her 'courage' (983), a word (*andreia*) which means literally 'manliness'. If, in her invitation to Chrysothemis, she says nothing about killing Clytaemnestra, this is not because she really means to kill only Aegisthus, or because she does not want to put her sister off. Rather, it is Sophocles who omits Clytaemnestra for the sake of the audience. We are to admire Electra for her great decision, and he is not yet ready for us to think about the horror of matricide. And admiration is the keynote of the choral song which follows.

The audience remains uncertain as to how the plot will develop. 'Will Electra launch a single-minded attack on the palace before Orestes makes his presence known?' (Budelmann). At this crucial moment Orestes and Pylades enter, and at last the recognition can take place. We may feel relieved that after all Electra will not have to act alone. Orestes carries the urn which is supposed to contain his ashes. She begs to hold it in her hands, and, as she weeps over it in intensely moving fashion, he comes to realise that his sister is before him. He gradually reveals his identity to Electra, and her joy is unrestrained. At this great emotional climax Electra expresses herself in song, while Orestes tries to restrain her in spoken iambic metre. All our attention is fixed on her. With superb irony, Electra, in whose hopes the return of Orestes and the act of vengeance had been inseparable, now forgets the vengeance altogether, until the Paedagogus arrives to insist, as he had insisted in the prologue, that the time for action has come. The audience has looked forward to the joy of recognition from the beginning of the play, and we too have put to the back of our minds the knowledge of what is still to come.

The three men enter the palace, while Electra remains on stage to pray for success to Apollo, the same god who had rejected Clytaemnestra's prayer for the death of her son. Then Electra too goes into the palace, leaving the stage for the first time since she entered it in the prologue. Will she, we wonder, take part in her mother's murder? But, after a brief excited song from the Chorus, she re-emerges to stand by the door, on guard against Aegisthus' arrival. We hear Clytaemnestra's death-shrieks offstage. Electra interprets for us what is happening inside the palace, and calls encouragement to her brother. Traditionally the matricide is Orestes' concern, but in this play, as he carries it out offstage, it is Electra whom we watch, so that she is still at the centre of our attention. The victorious Orestes emerges from the palace with the covered corpse. At this moment Aegisthus returns home, and at first takes the body to be that of Orestes. He discovers the truth, and the play ends with Orestes leading him into the palace to his death. It is all finished in just over a hundred lines.

Why is this final scene so short? On the answer to this question depends our whole interpretation of the tragedy. For some critics this is a happy play, and 'the horizon is free of all clouds' (Waldock); we rejoice with Orestes and Electra, and we feel that justice has been done, and the city has been rightly saved from the usurpers. In the traditional version of the story, followed by both Aeschylus and Euripides, Aegisthus is killed before Clytaemnestra, but in Sophocles Clytaemnestra is murdered first, so that her killing is not the last thing in our minds as we leave the theatre. And this too is why the scene is so short. Sophocles hurries over it so that it may not leave too deep an impression upon us. Wanting to write a happy play, but being constrained by his tradition to include a matricide, he does his best to ensure that no one notices it.

It is hard to believe what all of this implies, that Sophocles was not wholly in control of his material, or that in any culture matricide could be seen as unproblematic. Indeed, at various points in the play we have noted hints that the vengeance will not be morally straightforward. For other critics, therefore, 'this is a grim play' (Winnington-Ingram). Without going as far as Wheeler, who misinterprets Electra's great decision as a grave transgression and a mark of her derangement, we may still agree that the ending is far from happy. The justice of the killings and the legitimacy of Apollo's oracle may not be questioned (though we may note at 1424-5 the conditional clause in Orestes' 'all is well inside the house, *if* Apollo's prophecy was well spoken'), but we are surely struck by the horror. At 1415 Electra's cry to her offstage brother, 'Strike her a second blow, if you have the strength', is one of the nastiest lines in Greek tragedy. And, though we may not care much about the fate of Aegisthus, the way in which Orestes and Electra enjoy deceiving him is hardly pleasant. We may be inclined to believe him when, at 1498, he speaks of troubles still to come upon the family. The play ends as he is led away to die offstage, so that the killing carries on beyond the end.

The final scene is short and abrupt, not because Sophocles wants us not to notice it but because he wants to shock us. Everything has built up to the joyous recognition-scene, but immediately after it the mood changes dramatically. We suddenly realise what is still to come, and, far from suppressing the horror, Sophocles takes care to emphasise it. In the traditional story, as in Aeschylus and Euripides, Orestes is pursued by his mother's avenging Furies. There are no such Furies at the end of this play, but perhaps Sophocles intends us to take them for granted. Furies, indeed, have been mentioned at several points in the play (see e.g. p. 58), which would be surprising if they formed no part of his conception. The real reason why nothing is said about them at the end is that they traditionally concern only Orestes, and this is Electra's play, not his. We are not told what will happen now to Electra and Orestes, but we can hardly be sure that they will live happily ever after.

Philoctetes

Philoctetes is a tragedy about the effect of man's cruelty on man. On their way to Troy the Greek army stopped at the island of Chryse to make an offering to the goddess of the same name. Philoctetes, however, went too close to the altar, and was bitten in the foot by its guardian snake. The rest of the Greeks, finding his cries of pain and the smell from the wound unbearable, carried him over to the neighbouring island of Lemnos and abandoned him there. Nearly ten years later a Trojan prisoner, Helenus, prophesies that the Greeks will win the war only with the help of Philoctetes' invincible bow and arrows, the gift of Heracles. In Sophocles' version of the story Odysseus and the young Neoptolemus, the son of Achilles, are sent to fetch him, and the play opens with their arrival on Lemnos, which, by a dramatic convention which the audience easily accepts, is reckoned to be an uninhabited island.

Among the surviving plays of Sophocles *Philoctetes* is remarkable for the complexity of both its characterisation and its plot. We are presented with a tangle of relationships among all three men, Philoctetes, Neoptolemus and Odysseus, while Neoptolemus in particular is hardly less important a character than Philoctetes himself (some critics would argue that he is more important).

If Philoctetes is to be brought to Troy, to help those who abandoned him and whom he now considers to be his enemies, there are only three possible ways of securing him: he must be tricked or forced or persuaded. It is this that determines the structure of the play, which falls into three unequal parts, in each of which one of these methods is tried. The long first section is devoted to the attempt of Neoptolemus, coached by Odysseus, to deceive Philoctetes into going on board his ship, on the pretence that he means to take him home to Greece. At this stage the other two methods are simply dismissed (102-5) by Odysseus; Philoctetes hates the Greeks so much that he will never be persuaded, and violence cannot work as long as Philoctetes has in his hands the invincible bow. However, deceit in the end fails, and Odysseus, in the shortest of the three sections, has after all to resort to violence. But this too is unsuccessful, and the climax of the play takes the form of a series of attempts to *persuade* Philoctetes to come to Troy. The pressure on him gradually mounts, but in the end he resists all persuasion, and Neoptolemus agrees to take him, not to Troy, but home to Greece. It is only the intervention of Heracles, the *deus ex machina*, at the very end of the play, that causes Philoctetes to change his mind.

The complexity of the characterisation is probably one of the reasons that the Chorus, which consists of the crew of Neoptolemus' ship, is given so little to do in this play. Its entrance-song is shared with Neoptolemus, and in the whole play it sings only one formal ode (676-729). It is, however, by no means purely decorative. Apart from its obvious role of demonstrating loyalty to, and support for, Neoptolemus, it allows us to see him not simply as the young subordinate of Odysseus but as a commander of men in his own right. Moreover, at crucial points in the play, its attitude will have a crucial effect on our understanding of the mind of Neoptolemus himself.

It is the complexity of the plot that leads to one of the puzzles of the play: what exactly did the prophecy say? Did Helenus tell the Greeks that they must bring both Philoctetes and the bow, or would the bow by itself be enough, and did he say that he must be *persuaded* to come? If so, deceit and violence would seem to be ruled out from the very beginning. And did he prophesy that Philoctetes *would* go to Troy and that the Greeks would win the war, or that Troy would not fall *unless* Philoctetes were fetched? We may say, if we like, that the prophecy was somehow ambiguous, and that each character chose to interpret it according to what seemed to him to be the needs of the moment. We may then conclude that the final version, given by Neoptolemus near the end of the play, is the definitive one: Philoctetes *will* be persuaded to go to Troy, and the Greeks *will* win the war. But this is not real life, and it is better not to treat the prophecy as if there were an objective reality behind it. The three stages of the plot all depend on different conceptions of the prophecy, and it is Sophocles himself who had no compunction about varying its details to suit his dramatic purpose.

In the prologue we hear much about the environment of Philoctetes, the miserable cave in which he lives. Many Sophoclean heroes are in some way or another cut off from their society. On his uninhabited island Philoctetes is physically, as well as spiritually, isolated. It is this environment that has helped to make him what he has now become, and that will be a constant theme running through the play. Here, in the prologue, we see the environment before we see Philoctetes, the loneliness before the man, and our sympathy is already aroused. Odysseus explains to Neoptolemus his plan for tricking Philoctetes, and persuades him to play the major part in it. Odysseus cannot do so himself, because Philoctetes will at once recognise him as one of his greatest enemies. Neoptolemus is to pretend that the Greeks at Troy have robbed him of the arms of his father, Achilles, and in anger he has left the army and is now on his way home to Greece. Without the bow Troy will not be conquered (68-9); at this stage the prophecy appears to be conditional.

Neoptolemus, however, is hard to persuade. Deceit does not seem to him to be consistent with the heroic code which he has inherited from Achilles. The expression 'son of Achilles' will be heard throughout the play, always as a kind of symbol of Neoptolemus' better nature, whereas the names of Odysseus, and of Agamemnon and Menelaus, the sons of Atreus, will stand for all that is evil. The character of Odysseus has sadly deteriorated from his presentation in *Ajax*. It is now his cleverness, in the worst sense, that has come to the fore, and, if Neoptolemus favours an epic and slightly old-fashioned model of heroic nobility, Odysseus behaves like a late fifth-century sophist who uses clever rhetoric to gain his ends. For him the means are unimportant: 'when you are acting for gain, you should not hesitate' (111).

Neoptolemus is eventually persuaded by Odysseus' promise that if he co-operates he will gain a reputation for wisdom and at the same time for *arete* ('excellence'), the highest term of commendation for the Homeric hero (119). But he remains uneasy, and the conflict between his sense of duty to the army and his natural nobility will become clearer and clearer as the play progresses, until his true nature finally asserts itself. Vidal-Naquet and others have seen all this in terms of the initiation of a young man (an *ephebe*, see p. 56) into adult male Athenian society. The prologue ends with the departure of Odysseus, who promises to send a sailor to help Neoptolemus should he take too long to succeed in his mission.

In the lyric dialogue between the Chorus and Neoptolemus, which forms the entrance-song of the former, the Chorus guides our emotional response by expressing sympathy for Philoctetes, whom we have still to meet. Neoptolemus, while not unsympathetic, expresses the view that Philoctetes' sufferings are not surprising; they are all part of a divine plan to ensure that the invincible bow could not be used at Troy before the fated time had come for Troy to be captured. The conditional version of the prophecy is now dropped. Neoptolemus insists that Troy *will* fall. We may note that this is more than Odysseus told him in the prologue. It is almost as if he is trying to reassure himself that he has no responsibility in the matter; the gods know what they are doing, and all is for the best. His equivocation contrasts with the simple and sincere sympathy of his men.

At last Philoctetes enters, dragging his painful foot. He is overjoyed to discover that the stranger is Neoptolemus, the son of his old friend Achilles. He tells his pitiable story, not forgetting to mention (258) what upsets a hero more than anything else, the laughter of his enemies (see p. 13). Neoptolemus responds by telling his lying tale, convincing Philoctetes that they are both on the same side. Philoctetes questions Neoptolemus about the fortunes of his former colleagues at Troy. When he learns that the best of them are dead, while the villains survive, Philoctetes pours out his bitterness: why are the gods so unfair (446-52)? The speaker is, of course, Philoctetes, not Sophocles, but these lines are strangely overlooked by those who believe that the playwright's religion was one of simple, unquestioning piety. Neoptolemus expresses agreement with the other's sentiment (436-7, 456-7). This is no doubt part of the deceit, but we suspect that, ironically, in his heart of hearts he is really closer to Philoctetes than he is to Odysseus. At the same time the exchange demonstrates Philoctetes' loyalty to the good men, whom he considers to be his friends. Supported by the Chorus, he begs Neoptolemus to take him on his ship to Greece, and the latter, after a show of reluctance, agrees to do so. Odysseus' plan seems to have worked.

At this moment, however, two men arrive. They are the sailor promised by (and played by the same actor as) Odysseus in the prologue, and his companion. The sailor is disguised as the captain of a merchant-ship, and by the end of the scene everything is changed. At 431-2 Neoptolemus has remarked that 'even clever plans are often thwarted'. In the words of Robert Burns, 'the best laid schemes o' mice an' men gang aft agley'. With splendid Sophoclean irony it is Odysseus' clever scheme for hastening his plan that will begin to sway Neoptolemus against it and ultimately cause it to fail. The Merchant pretends to reveal to Neoptolemus that he must leave as quickly as possible, because two parties of Greeks are on their way, the one to bring back Neoptolemus to Troy, the other, consisting of Diomedes and Odysseus, to fetch Philoctetes. The Merchant repeats the prophecy of Helenus (again it is conditional – Troy will not fall unless ...), but adds a new piece of information: Philoctetes has to be brought in person (so the bow by itself will not be sufficient), and he must be *persuaded* to come.

Philoctetes, who has heard the whole conversation between the other two, now knows for the first time that there is a plan to bring him to Troy. The effect on him is predictable. Now that he is faced with the arrival of his enemies, we see for the first time his strength of will and the depth of his hatred. He would as soon be persuaded to come back from the dead as to go to Troy to help his enemies (623-5). Persuasion can, therefore, be ruled out as impossible. Much more subtle is the effect that the scene has on Neoptolemus. After the Merchant's departure Philoctetes calls on his new friend to set sail immediately with him for Greece, but Neoptolemus wants to delay: 'when the headwind drops, then we shall set out; for now it is against us' (639-40). Sophocles' audience did not need a map to tell it that, if the wind was against a ship sailing south-west towards Greece, it was an ideal wind for one heading for Troy. Neoptolemus' excuse is a sign of his inner torment, and the first clear indication that the deception is going to fail. Philoctetes, however, for the moment overrules him, and the two men go into the cave to collect his few belongings in preparation for departure.

The Chorus, left alone in the orchestra, sings the only formal ode in this play. It dwells again, with sympathy, on the background to Philoctetes' sufferings, but the final stanza presents a puzzle; Philoctetes, it sings, will now be relieved of all his troubles; for he is going home to Greece. Either it has temporarily forgotten Philoctetes' real destination, or, more probably, since the latter is now within earshot the Chorus has to resume the pretence.

As the two men prepare to depart to the ship Philoctetes has a sudden attack of pain, which can be alleviated, he explains, only if he goes to sleep. He hands over the precious bow to Neoptolemus for safe-keeping while he sleeps. It is only now, when the latter has the bow in his hands, that the exact wording of the prophecy becomes an important issue. If the bow, without its owner, is sufficient, Neoptolemus is now free to depart, abandoning Philo-ctetes to his fate, robbed of the bow on which he relied to shoot birds for his food. The tension for the audience is immediately increased by the Chorus when it urges its commander to do precisely what we are afraid that he will do. This is certainly not to the Chorus' credit, but the characterisation of the Chorus is not the important issue. What matters is that the failure in its sympathy is balanced by a further increase in the sympathy of Neoptolemus (in the entrance-song it was the other way round; see p. 68). He insists that the bow by itself is not enough, and that Philoctetes himself must be brought. The Chorus is not convinced. The difference may simply be one of interpreting a prophecy that was vague on details. Some critics suppose that Neoptolemus here reveals a new, and better, understanding. But it is hard to see where that new understanding comes from. The Merchant has mentioned persuasion, but the Merchant is a liar, and Neoptolemus says nothing about persuasion here. The important point is that Neoptolemus refuses to play the shabby trick recommended by his men. He is beginning to return to his true self.

Philoctetes on awakening is full of gratitude to his friend for standing by him, but Neoptolemus is now in an agony of indecision. 'What am I to do?' he cries, like so many tragic heroes. Eventually he blurts out that he is taking Philoctetes not to Greece but to Troy. This has to be, he says (921-6); it is his duty. It is also expedient for him, so the end still justifies the means. There is, then, some way to go before he finally gives in to Philoctetes' appeals. In an impassioned speech Philoctetes begs Neoptolemus to give him back his bow. He curses the 'son of Achilles' (940) and, when the latter remains silent (934-5, 951), appeals to the Lemnian landscape, the constant background to his tragedy. He begs Neoptolemus at least to give him back his bow. Again the latter cries, 'What am I to do?' (969, 974). At the very moment when he is evidently advancing across the stage to return the bow, Odysseus makes a remarkably abrupt entry, in time to foil Neoptolemus' act of generosity.

At last the two enemies confront each other, and we move into the short second stage, in which Odysseus attempts force. Philoctetes threatens to commit suicide, and Odysseus has him seized to prevent it. But then he releases him, on the grounds that now they have the bow, and that is all they need. In all of this Neoptolemus speaks not a word, until the very end, when he gives the Chorus permission to remain behind temporarily, in the hope that Philoctetes may change his mind, while he and Odysseus depart to prepare for sailing.

Odysseus must really believe that the bow by itself is sufficient. Some critics have thought that Odysseus, in releasing Philoctetes, shows a new awareness that persuasion, not violence, is required; he still hopes that Neoptolemus will somehow be successful, and allows the Chorus to begin the process of persuasion. If so, the new awareness comes remarkably suddenly. For others the threat to abandon Philoctetes is merely bluff. Odysseus is confident that, when he realises what he is losing, Philoctetes will come running after him. But, apart from being over-subtle, this would ruin the tension which will underlie the following lyric dialogue between Philoctetes and the Chorus. The audience must believe that there is a real possibility that he will be abandoned on Lemnos without his bow. At the same time, we do not want him to become untrue to himself by yielding to his enemies.

In the lyric dialogue the Chorus shows sympathy for Philoctetes in his plight, but tells him that it is in his own power to put an end to it by going to Troy. The final, climactic, stage is thus prepared. Neoptolemus and Odysseus reappear, the former with the intention of returning the bow to Philoctetes. With a new-found self-confidence and authority, he soon discomfits the horrified Odysseus, and hands over the bow to the astonished Philoctetes. Odysseus cannot stop him, and makes his final exit. Neoptolemus has at last shown himself worthy of his father Achilles (1310-13).

It is now time for us to concentrate on the method of persuasion, and on the idea that Philoctetes must go willingly to Troy (1332). Already at 919-20 Neoptolemus had pointed out that it was in Philoctetes' interests to go to Troy, where he would be saved from his misery and would share in the glory of winning the war. Even Odysseus, in the midst of his violence, had used the latter argument (997-8), but with no hope of success. In the lyric dialogue the Chorus too has tried persuasion, and at least it was sympathetic to Philoctetes. But it is only Neoptolemus, now that he has proved himself to be a true friend, who can apply persuasion effectively.

According to Helenus' prophecy, he says, Troy *will* fall this summer (1340-1). Not only will Philoctetes have the glory of capturing
it; there are also doctors there, the sons of Asclepius, who can cure
the wound in his foot. Philoctetes is strongly tempted; he understands what he is missing, just as earlier (1125) he has pictured the
laughter of Odysseus with the bow in his hands. It is now Philoctetes' turn to cry, 'What shall I do?' He wants to co-operate with
his friend, but in the end it is his wish to harm his enemies that
triumphs over his obligation to help his friends (for the opposite
decision see p. 19). As the typical Sophoclean hero, he refuses,
therefore, to learn sense or to yield. In the first stage of the play
deceit, by its very nature, could make no impact on his will. In the
second stage violence could affect him only externally. But this
third stage involves a fundamental struggle for his character, as we
see him facing, but resisting, the strongest pressure to do what he
feels to be wrong.

That the audience is meant to admire Philoctetes for his decision
is shown by the fact that, having returned to his true self, Neoptolemus finally agrees to take him home to Greece. The effect of
Philoctetes on Neoptolemus is ultimately important for what it tells
us about Philoctetes. We may compare in *Ajax* the recognition by
Odysseus of the heroic stature of Ajax (see p. 19). The point is
important for the interpretation of the final 63 lines of the play. Just
as it seemed to be coming to an end, with the two men preparing to
depart for Greece, that departure is abruptly and surprisingly inter-
rupted by the appearance of the deified Heracles, the previous
owner of the bow and the friend of Philoctetes. In his role of *deus
ex machina*, the only one in Sophocles' surviving plays, he orders
them to fulfil the purpose of Zeus by going instead to Troy, where
Philoctetes will be healed and, together with Neoptolemus, win
the glory of capturing the city. Philoctetes agrees to go. His
sudden change of mind may disappoint us, and we may think of
a modern film in which the script-writer has tacked a happy
ending onto a novel which originally ended tragically. Why does
Sophocles do it?

It may be simply that the original audience, familiar with the traditional story, knew that Philoctetes *did* go to Troy and that the Greeks did win the war. Somehow Sophocles had to reconcile his tragedy with the story as the audience knew it. In that sense the ending was 'fated', but it requires a miracle to bring it about.

More important, the 'second' ending raises the question of Philoctetes' status as a hero. Heracles, who had won glory after suffering, and who had received divine status after death, serves as a kind of prototype for Philoctetes himself. He does not condemn him, either for committing sacrilege on Chryse or for his refusal to accept his destiny. He merely commands him, and states what is going to happen. Philoctetes will not become a god, but his recognition by the gods, and the glory that awaits him, mean that his heroic greatness is assured. There may even be a hint of a future hero-cult on Chryse, although the evidence for this is late. Harrison puts it well: 'Philoctetes … like the Oedipus of *Oedipus Coloneus* combines physical infirmity with grand passions and sufferings which transcend the measure of mortality and suggest daemonic stature.' Similarly in *Ajax* it was the burial of the hero that restored him to his heroic status (see p. 17).

The 'second' ending of the play is, then, a happy one. But it is not entirely happy, and the play remains a tragedy. The divine plan hardly seems to justify the suffering that it involves. Philoctetes will return to society, but the cruel Odysseus, Agamemnon and Menelaus have not changed, and Philoctetes never secures the justice for which he has longed; instead, his enemies will get what they want.

In his final words Heracles warns against impiety, and we may recall the brutality of Neoptolemus who, according to the tradition, will kill Priam at an altar. In his last speech Philoctetes addresses the landscape of Lemnos, looking not forward to the glory that awaits him but back, to the scene of his sufferings, the environment to which we were introduced at the beginning of the play.

Oedipus at Colonus

This play deals with the end of Oedipus' life, and thus comes chronologically between the events presented in *Oedipus the King* and in *Antigone*. Probably many years separate the three plays from each other, and it is unhelpful to think of them as a 'Theban trilogy', as if they were conceived as a unity, and written for a single continuous performance. Each has its own dramatic purpose, and one should resist the temptation to interpret one in terms of another.

Two differences may be mentioned. The role of Creon, a character in all three plays, is different in each. First, in *Antigone* he is a king who means well, but who, apparently for the best of motives, deludes himself into thinking that wrong is right; in *Oedipus the King* he is an honest, decent, though not very admirable man, who does his best for Oedipus at the end; while in *Oedipus at Colonus* he is an unscrupulous villain, worthy to be equated with the Odysseus of *Philoctetes*. Secondly, the problem of Oedipus' guilt and responsibility, which bulked so large in *Oedipus the King*, has ceased to be an issue in this last play. Oedipus now insists, at three points in the play, that he is morally innocent because his crimes were committed in ignorance, and that in any case his killing of the stranger at the place where three roads met was a lawful act of self-defence. He now regrets his self-blinding. It is not that at the end of his life Sophocles believes that he has found a simple answer to a question which had earlier seemed so intractable. Rather, Oedipus' assertion of his innocence is Sophocles' way of telling us that he has other concerns now than the question of responsibility.

Oedipus at Colonus presents the transformation of Oedipus into a 'hero', in the Greek sense of that word – a man who after death is granted a status between that of god and mortal, and who will be honoured by the living with a cult.

At the beginning of the play he arrives with his faithful companion, Antigone, at the grove of the Eumenides, the 'Kindly Goddesses', at Colonus near Athens, the birthplace of Sophocles himself. He is a helpless, blind old man, and he arouses first the horror of the stranger of Colonus who finds him trespassing on holy ground, and then the much deeper horror of the Chorus of old men of Colonus when it arrives and discovers that he is the notorious and polluted outcast, Oedipus. Yet it has already appeared that this helpless old man has certain knowledge. The oracle which so long ago predicted that he would kill his father and marry his mother told him also that he would one day find rest near such a seat of the Eumenides, who, under another name, are the Furies, the Erinyes. His body is to be a source of blessing to those who receive him, and a source of trouble for those who have cast him out of Thebes. The theme of friends and enemies is clearly going to be important in this play, as in others. Nothing was said about this prophecy in *Oedipus the King*; the oracle has changed to suit the requirements of the new play.

In one sense, however, the beginning of *Oedipus at Colonus* mirrors its predecessor; for the blind and helpless, but spiritually-sighted, Oedipus reminds us of Teiresias in *Oedipus the King*. There his vaunted human wisdom had turned out to be ignorance. Now, as this play proceeds, and as Oedipus is eventually granted asylum by King Theseus, the favourite Athenian hero, it becomes more and more evident that in this play his knowledge and wisdom are very real. 'All that I say I shall say with vision', he tells the Stranger in the prologue (74). When the time comes for him to depart, summoned by the thunder, no longer leaning on Antigone's arm, he himself, the blind man, leads Theseus and his daughters from the stage, and we learn from the Messenger how the gods finally took him to themselves, how he disappeared from sight, with only Theseus to preserve the secret of his resting-place. His passing is impressive and mysterious. The whole play is full of religious awe and sanctity, from the description of the grove of the Eumenides in the prologue, through the ritual for Oedipus' atonement for trespassing on that grove, to the final climactic scene.

On a superficial level the play seems easy to interpret. *Oedipus the King* presented the passing of a man from the height of prosperity and success to ruin. Here the process is reversed, as we watch him pass from misery and weakness to glory and triumph. Aristotle, in his discussion of the different types of tragic plot in his *Poetics*, does not even consider the possibility of a tragedy in which a good man passes from unhappiness to happiness. A modern reader too may have doubts about a tragedy which apparently ends so happily.

The structure of the play is also very different from that of *Oedipus the King*. There is no Aristotelian 'reversal' or 'recognition'. Its plot seems to be what Aristotle would call 'simple', in that it progresses in a gradual and straightforward manner to an end that was already foreseen at the beginning. It appears too to be much looser in construction. There are two scenes which seem to break the orderly progression to the appointed end, the first (prepared by the arrival of Antigone's sister Ismene) in which Creon arrives in the vain hope of persuading Oedipus to return with him to Thebes, and thus be a source of blessing to that city; the second in which his son Polyneices comes, equally vainly, to seek his father's blessing in the coming struggle with his brother Eteocles for the throne of Thebes; whichever side Oedipus supports will win.

The plot has, not surprisingly, been labelled episodic, the kind of 'simple' plot which Aristotle seems to have disliked the most. Consider in particular the moment in which Creon has Antigone carried off as a hostage by his men, to join Ismene whom, he tells us, he has already captured, and is prevented only by the arrival of Theseus from laying hands on Oedipus himself. This is a moment of excitement and violence, uncommon in Sophoclean drama, but what is its relevance to the plot? Is it merely, as Waldock says, 'a gripping interlude'?

And what are we to make of the praise of Athens which pervades the play? One thinks especially of the famous ode at 668-719, in which the Chorus pays tribute to all the varied aspects of Attic life. It is one of the most beautiful of all Sophocles' songs, and no doubt it would give much pleasure to his Athenian audience. But what has it to do with the play? Is it simply the work of an old man, weary after many years of the Peloponnesian War, and looking back with longing to Athens as it used to be, or perhaps seeking to bolster his fellow-citizens' morale at a critical period in their national fortunes? How too should we regard the almost equally famous ode at 1211-48, in which the Chorus dwells upon the miseries of old age? Is the aged Sophocles merely using the Chorus as the mouthpiece for his own personal complaints?

If we look closely at the construction of the plot we may decide that it is not after all so simple, and that the ending of the play is not as happy as it seemed at first sight. Over against the straightforward progression from misery to glory Sophocles has set another movement, one of increasing violence and foreboding.

Oedipus, like every Sophoclean hero, has to face a series of attacks on his resolution. First he has to overcome the horror of the old man of Colonus who wants to remove him from the sanctuary. Next he has to persuade the Chorus to let him stay. But the main problem is presented first by Creon and then by Polyneices, both of them anxious to secure his person for their own advantage.

The two scenes in which we meet them form a dramatic climax. The villainous Creon tries three methods, deceit, violence, and persuasion, a pattern that Sophocles has already used in *Philoctetes*. Oedipus has little difficulty in disposing of him. He has already learnt from Ismene (399-400) that Creon's offer to bring him home is not sincere; he is to be established *outside* Theban territory, in a place where he can be controlled. Theseus goes off with his men to rescue the kidnapped girls, and successfully restores them to their father.

Polyneices will be more difficult. Oedipus does not want to receive the suppliant at all, but he yields to the persuasion of Antigone, who is so much softer and more human than himself. Oedipus blames his sons for his exile. Polyneices, who begins by pitying his father's helpless state, now says that he is sorry, but Oedipus is utterly relentless. Instead of blessing his son, he utters, as he did earlier at 421-7, a terrible curse against the two brothers, which, as we know, will be fulfilled when they kill each other in single combat. This is the angry Oedipus whom we encountered in *Oedipus the King*. He may now perhaps be using his anger in the service of the gods, but the fact remains that this Oedipus, in his towering rage, cursing his own family, is a much less attractive figure than his own daughter Antigone, who has words of sympathy for Polyneices: 'Wretched am I', she says (1442-3), 'if I am to be deprived of you.' Polyneices reciprocates her love.

According to the Greek moral code one should help one's friends and relations (*philoi*) and harm one's enemies (*echthroi*), and we have seen (pp. 12, 40) that tragedy often arises when the characters confuse these categories. So here Antigone and Polyneices treat each other as *philoi*, and the mutual love between Oedipus and his daughters is very real. But this serves only to intensify by contrast Oedipus' bitter relationship with his sons, whom he treats as *echthroi*. Nowhere else in surviving tragedy is such a formal supplication rejected. So Polyneices goes off, hoping that the curse will not be fulfilled, just as Oedipus in former days had hoped that Apollo's oracle would never come to pass. As the play ends there is tragedy ahead, not only for Polyneices and Eteocles, but also for the innocent Antigone and Ismene.

It is because there are two contrary movements in the play that we have such contrasts of mood. Indeed it is these contrasts that provide the structure of the play. Each is carefully contrived. The first part of the play builds up to Theseus' courteous granting of asylum to Oedipus. This is followed by the Colonus ode, in which the Chorus praises Colonus and Attica, the land which has given asylum to Oedipus, and which will prosper as a result. The mood is one of beauty and peace. Then Creon enters, and from the peace of Athens we are thrown into the turmoil of Thebes. The kidnapping of the two girls is exciting, but it is not excitement for its own sake. It is the anger and the violence themselves that matter, in contrast with the peace that has gone before. The girls are duly returned to Oedipus, but the joy is only momentary. Theseus brings news of the arrival of Polyneices, and we prepare for a still angrier scene. Before he enters the Chorus sings its ode on the miseries of old age. This too is relevant. The troubles which it describes may soon be over for Oedipus, but they are not over yet. Its picture of fighting and strife is an appropriate prelude to the Polyneices scene. That scene is both parallel with, and an intensification of, the Creon scene. In the latter we saw Oedipus refusing to help his country, but now we see him cursing his own family. He has won rest and friendship in Athens, but at the cost of eternal enmity with his own native city and with his family.

The final contrast of the play is the most dramatic of all. The religious exaltation and the mysterious splendour of Oedipus' passing do not mark the end of the play. What comes last is the lamentation of the sisters, and their fears for themselves and the future of the family. It is the story of *Antigone* that is in our minds as the play comes to its end. Oedipus' curse will destroy Antigone, whom he loves, as well as those he hates. So the movement towards Oedipus' glory is matched throughout by a contrary movement that leads towards the further ruination of the house. *Oedipus the King* ends on a note of hope, but *Oedipus at Colonus* on one of pessimism.

Still, the audience no doubt rejoices that Oedipus has won his rest, and the gods have granted him recognition as a hero. We may wonder why they have done so. Is it that they have decided to make amends to him for his past sufferings, a view perhaps underlying the words of the Chorus at 1565-7, 'for though many troubles came upon him without cause, a just god may lift him up again'. The gods, according to some critics, having (belatedly?) realised that Oedipus was after all morally innocent in killing his father and marrying his mother, now do their best to make it up to him. But we saw on p. 75 that the question of his moral responsibility is not a major issue in this play. Some scholars have found in it a general, and pious, theological statement about the justice of the gods.

'Oedipus' individual destiny', says Bowra, 'is an example of the gods' ultimate justice to men'. But it does not seem to be because Oedipus is good that the gods reward him. At the beginning of the play he gives an impression of a humility that was largely lacking in *Oedipus the King*: 'my sufferings and the long passage of time, my companion, and thirdly my nobility, teach me patience' (7-8), and indeed he seems quite unheroic. But his old character soon reasserts itself, and for most of the play he is as stubborn and bad-tempered as ever. Nor is there any sign that the gods love Oedipus or show tenderness towards him. As Kirkwood says, the grace in this play is human grace, the grace which we see in the new relationship between Oedipus and Theseus, a highly sympathetic character who may remind us of Odysseus in *Ajax*. There is little softness in the gods or in heroes like Oedipus. As so often in Sophocles' plays, we may admire the hero, while finding other characters more attractive, and we ourselves could never hope to emulate him. We shall not be given the status of 'heroes' when we die.

What the gods recognise in Oedipus is, then, not his moral goodness but his moral endurance, his strength of spirit, and his integrity, the qualities for which we too, as the audience, admire him. Already in his earlier plays Sophocles has experimented with different ways of granting some kind of recognition to his heroes. In *Ajax* the granting of burial to the hero marked that recognition. In *Antigone* the admission of Creon that he was wrong assures us that Antigone was right to bury her brother. In *Philoctetes*, the play closest in date to *Oedipus at Colonus*, it is the epiphany of Heracles that promises the hero glory. At the end of *Oedipus the King* there is little reassurance for the future, but at least Oedipus has remained true to himself and has now acquired what he values most, true knowledge and understanding. Nowhere is this idea more clearly expressed than in *Oedipus at Colonus*, where it is in our minds from the very beginning of the play. Oedipus has maintained his integrity, and at the end he becomes a 'hero' in the Greek sense of that word.

Oedipus, then, has his reward, not indeed the promise of a blessed existence in paradise, but the promise of a cult and the power to harm his enemies and help his new friends, a valuable power in the eyes of the Greeks. This is the culmination of the principal movement of the play. But Sophocles gives no answer (how could he?) to the problem of why throughout his life he had to endure such suffering. And, as we have seen, it is with the other movement that the play ends. We are brought down from religious mysticism to the world of human concerns, as we look forward to the continuing tragedy of Oedipus' family. As always in Sophocles, the optimism and the pessimism are finely mixed. But it is clearly an over-simplification to describe *Oedipus at Colonus* as a 'happy' play.

Epilogue

As the younger contemporary of Aeschylus and the older contemporary of Euripides (who died before him), and as the favourite tragedian of Aristotle, whose theory of the best kind of tragedy is based largely on *Oedipus the King*, Sophocles has always occupied a central position in the study of Greek tragedy. With a reputation in antiquity for religious piety, and apparently exempt from the satire inflicted on Aeschylus and Euripides by fifth-century comedy, he has often, until comparatively recent times, been praised as a fine example of Classical perfection, a model of reason and enlightenment, worthy, in his own sphere, to be compared with the Parthenon and all the other achievements of Periclean Athens. In books written a few decades ago he appears as a political and religious conformist, a pious believer in the gods, a man for whom the highest virtue is *sophrosyne* (moderation, discipline, self-control), and who wrote his plays to inculcate in his fellow-citizens that dullest of all virtues. If all this were true, we should have to characterise Sophocles as someone who did not have much to say, but who managed to say it in fine poetry in well-constructed plays.

More recently scholarly attitudes to Sophocles have changed. Scholars, on the whole, are less eager to look for simple morals or messages in Greek tragedy in general, and in the particular case of Sophocles they have come to recognise that the tragic vision which he presents is a good deal more complex and profound than their predecessors were willing to acknowledge. It is true that much is said about *sophrosyne* in his plays, but it is usually the ordinary mediocre people, or the secondary characters, or the chorus, who advocate it, often in the most platitudinous of forms, and sometimes, as with Menelaus in *Ajax*, it is a villain who sings its praises.

Usually we hear of *sophrosyne* in the context of an attempt at persuading the self-centred hero to change his mind, to compromise, to learn common-sense, to yield to forces that are stronger than himself or herself. The Sophoclean hero always refuses to do so, and it is the Sophoclean hero whom Sophocles forces us to admire.

Some recent critics have warned us against a 'hero-worshipping' approach to Sophocles, and yet some at least of his characters (Ajax, Oedipus, perhaps Philoctetes) *were* worshipped in Greek hero-cult, as men who after death were raised to a status between that of man and god, while Heracles actually became a god. So far, however, as the plays themselves are concerned, to say that we admire a character should not imply that Sophocles intends us to worship him, or to set him up as a role-model for us lesser mortals. 'In ordinary life we seek, so far as lies in our power, to keep ourselves remote from tragedy, but we also stay remote from greatness, aspiring to the condition of a Creon and not an Oedipus' (Winnington-Ingram). The secondary characters, such as Ismene or Chrysothemis, or Jocasta, are often more attractive, while the hero, one feels, would be impossible to live with. In almost every play the hero, by his very nature, is in one way or another isolated from, and presents problems for, his society. This was doubtless a matter of particular concern for the fifth-century Athenian democratic audience, for whom outstanding men were naturally suspect. In that sense the plays are political (from time to time attempts have been made to identify specific Athenian statesmen as the models for Sophocles' characters, but none have commanded much assent; uncertainty about the dating of the plays makes such attempts particularly hazardous). Yet even Athenian society needed and admired its 'heroes'.

In ancient literary criticism the word 'hero' is never used to designate the principal character of a play. It is, however, hard to deny that, although no Sophoclean play is a doublet of another, in all of them there is a character who stands out, to a greater or lesser degree, from the rest in the way described above. This is most obvious in the two Oedipus plays, and in *Electra*, where Orestes does little more than provide the framework for Electra's tragedy. In these plays the presentation of the minor characters is all intended to illuminate, by contrast, that of the principal character. It is less obvious in those plays in which we find another character, not really minor at all, whom Sophocles has made almost as interesting as the 'hero' – Creon in *Antigone*, Deianeira in *Women of Trachis*, Odysseus in *Ajax*, in all of which the characters illuminate one another. This double focus can affect a play's construction, and it has led some critics to label such plays unhelpfully as 'diptych-plays'. From this point of view *Philoctetes* is the most complicated play of all, as we watch the interaction of the three main characters, Philoctetes, Neoptolemus and Odysseus. Some critics have even been tempted to suppose that Creon, not Antigone, is the principal character of *Antigone*, Deianeira of *Women of Trachis*, and Neoptolemus of *Philoctetes*. It is better to recognise that Sophocles could write tragedies in which there is no one hero, but which are concerned entirely with relationships between two or more characters. And yet, in every case one of the two (or three) characters stands out by behaving in the manner which I have described as that of the typical Sophoclean hero, while the other behaves differently – more attractively perhaps, but also less heroically. No play presents a conflict between two equally characterised heroes. That Odysseus agrees to Ajax's burial is a measure of the latter's greatness, rather than his own, while Neoptolemus' decision to take Philoctetes home is a confirmation that the latter was right to refuse to yield to Odysseus.

It would be an exaggeration to say that the Sophoclean hero suffers *because of* his greatness, but one may certainly feel that if he had not been great he might have avoided his suffering. If Antigone had been more like Ismene, would it really have mattered? As Aristotle well understood, the greater and the more prosperous the hero, the more striking is his fall. Why then does he suffer? Sometimes it is because of other people's mistakes or cruelty, sometimes because of his insistence on doing what he believes to be right, sometimes because of his own mistakes. He never falls because he is wicked. If one asks why he makes mistakes, Sophocles' answer would seem to be that this is just the way that things are, and there is nothing that we can do about it. Only the gods are omniscient. Human beings, by virtue of their very humanity, never attain to full understanding. Sooner or later they are bound to make a mistake, a mistake which may lead to suffering and even tragedy, for themselves and other people. They cannot avoid making their mistakes, and yet they must accept responsibility for the consequences.

The idea that we live in a world of appearances, and often illusion, is related to the tragic irony which is so characteristic of Sophocles' plays. The characters may think that everything is going well, but the audience, which, like the gods themselves, knows the truth, sees that they are moving ever closer to disaster. Irony is evident in most of Sophocles' tragedies, for example in *Antigone* where Creon, in his aim to be a good king, ends up by bringing pollution on his city and losing his own wife and son, and in *Women of Trachis*, where Deianeira, in her plan to reignite her husband's love succeeds only in destroying them both. But in no play does it so dominate the plot as in *Oedipus the King*. Oedipus sets out to save his city, and ruins himself. He curses the unknown murderers of Laius, and so curses himself. Jocasta tries to reassure her husband in his anxiety, but instead makes him more worried. The Corinthian Messenger tries to reassure him by revealing that Polybus was not his father, and thus inadvertently leads to the full revelation of the dreadful truth.

Why the world of human beings is so imperfect Sophocles makes no attempt to explain. How could he? The great problems of human life are, as Goethe once said, insoluble; if they could be solved, there would be no tragedy. Sophocles' reputation for piety has already been mentioned, and there is certainly no reason to doubt that he believed in the existence of the gods. But that does not mean that he accepts them unquestioningly, or that he finds much comfort in their dealings with mortals. Their ways are inscrutable for human beings. Athena in the prologue of *Ajax* maintains that the gods love those who practise *sophrosyne*, but we have seen reason to doubt her sincerity, and, in any case, we have to set such a statement against the bewilderment of Philoctetes as to why the gods have allowed the best men to die at Troy, while the wicked have survived. Deianeira and Ismene receive no reward for their *sophrosyne*. We would all like to live in a world in which virtuous people (like ourselves) are guaranteed prosperity, happiness, and success, while wicked people (our enemies) meet with their just deserts. It is this longing that underlies the difficult ode in *Oedipus the King* (p. 51), in which the Chorus searches desperately for a connection between morality and success in life.

Sophocles' plays contain no simple lessons, and we should beware of looking for them in the choral odes. The Chorus, usually but not always (*Antigone*) composed of supporters of the principal character, can be just as blind and mistaken as everyone else. Its function is to create atmosphere and mood, often through the medium of beautiful poetry (as in the Colonus ode in *Oedipus at Colonus*, or, in the same play, the ode on the miseries of old age), and to ensure that we ask the right questions about the tragedy as it unfolds. It guides, then, both our emotional and our intellectual response to the action.

It would be wrong to suppose that Sophocles' plays all end on a note of utter despair. Usually something has been gained. Oedipus has lost his kingdom, his wife, and his sight, but he has achieved that which he values most – knowledge and understanding. Ajax has his funeral and is restored to his status as a hero, while Philoctetes will be restored to health and will share with Neoptolemus the glory for capturing Troy. Moreover, in various ways Sophocles almost always leaves us with a feeling of admiration for the heights to which his heroes can rise. But even in the plays which may seem to have a 'happy' ending the happiness is by no means unalloyed. In *Electra* it is not the joy of the recognition but the horror of the murders that ends the play. In *Women of Trachis* we may look forward to the apotheosis of Heracles, but little stress is laid on it in the final scene. Nor can we ever forget the suffering that has gone before, or, at least in *Oedipus at Colonus*, the suffering that is still to come, and there are too many uncertainties for our comfort. A blend of optimism and pessimism is characteristic of Sophoclean tragedy.

Suggestions for Further Reading

Texts, Commentaries and Translations

All the plays may be found in two volumes in the Loeb Classical Library, edited, with introduction, Greek text, and English translation, by H. Lloyd-Jones (1994). The following individual plays appear in the Aris & Phillips series (Warminster), with introduction, Greek text and English translation, and with a commentary based not on the Greek text but on the translation: *Ajax*, A.F. Garvie (1998); *Antigone*, A. Brown (1987); *Electra*, J. March (2001); *Philoctetes*, R.G. Ussher (1990). The following editions in the Cambridge Greek and Latin Classics series are intended primarily for readers who know Greek, but at least their introductions are generally accessible to Greekless readers: *Women of Trachis* (*Trachiniae*), P.E. Easterling (1982); *Antigone*, M. Griffith (1999); *Oedipus the King* (*Oedipus Rex*), R.D. Dawe (1982); *Electra*, J.H. Kells (1973); *Philoctetes*, T.B.L. Webster (1970). J. Wilkins and M. Macleod, *Sophocles' Antigone & Oedipus the King* (Bristol Classical Press 1987) is a commentary based on the English translation of R. Fagles (Penguin 1984).

Books

The following list is highly selective, and is restricted to those titles in which a knowledge of the language is not essential, most or all of the Greek being translated into English.

(a) General

Easterling, P.E. (ed.), *The Cambridge Companion to Greek Tragedy* (Cambridge 1997).
Heath, M., *The Poetics of Greek Tragedy* (London 1987).
Kitto, H.D.F., *Form and Meaning in Drama: a Study of Six Greek*

Plays and of Hamlet (London 1956): especially *Ajax*, *Antigone*, *Philoctetes*.

————— *Greek Tragedy* (3rd edn London 1961).

Rehm, R., *Greek Tragic Theatre* (London 1992).

Taplin, O., *Greek Tragedy in Action* (London 1978): especially *Ajax, Oedipus the King, Philoctetes.*

(b) Sophocles

Bernidaki-Aldous, E.A., *Blindness in a Culture of Light: Especially the Case of* Oedipus at Colonus *of Sophocles* (New York, Berne, Frankfurt am Main, Paris 1990).

Blundell, M.W., *Helping Friends and Harming Enemies: a Study in Sophocles and Greek Ethics* (Cambridge 1989).

Budelmann, F., *The Language of Sophocles: Communality, Communication and Involvement* (Cambridge 2000).

Buxton, R.G.A., *Sophocles* (*Greece & Rome* New Surveys in the Classics, Oxford 1995).

Gellie, G., *Sophocles: a Reading* (Melbourne 1972).

Hesk, J., *Sophocles: Ajax* (Duckworth Companions to Greek and Roman Tragedy, London 2003).

Kirkwood, G.M., *A Study of Sophoclean Drama* (Cornell 1958).

Knox, B.M.W., *The Heroic Temper: Studies in Sophoclean Tragedy* (California 1964).

Musurillo, H., *The Light and the Darkness: Studies in the Dramatic Poetry of Sophocles* (Leiden 1967).

Scodel, R., *Sophocles* (Twayne's World Author Series, Boston 1984).

Seale, D., *Vision and Stagecraft in Sophocles* (London and Canberra 1982).

Segal, C., *Tragedy and Civilization: an Interpretation of Sophocles* (Cambridge, MA 1981).

————— *Sophocles' Tragic World: Divinity, Nature, Society* (Cambridge, MA 1995).

Tyrrell, W.B. and Bennett, L.J., *Recapturing Sophocles' Antigone* (Lanham, Boulder, New York, Oxford 1998).

Whitman, C.H., *Sophocles: a Study of Heroic Humanism* (Cambridge, MA 1951).

Winnington-Ingram. R.P., *Sophocles: an Interpretation* (Cambridge 1980).

Other scholars mentioned by name in the text

Belfiore, E.S., *Murder among Friends: Violation of* philia *in Greek Tragedy* (Oxford 2000).

Bowra, C.M., *Sophoclean Tragedy* (Oxford 1944).

Foley, H.P., 'Antigone as moral agent', in M.S. Silk (ed.) *Tragedy and the Tragic: Greek Theatre and Beyond* (Oxford 1996), 49-73.

Harrison, S.J., 'Sophocles and the cult of Philoctetes', *Journal of Hellenic Studies* 109 (1989), 173-5.

March, J.R., 'Sophocles' *Ajax*: the death and burial of a hero', *Bulletin of the Institute of Classical Studies* 38 (1991-3), 1-36.

Seaford, R., 'The tragic wedding', *Journal of Hellenic Studies* 107 (1987), 106-30.

——— 'The imprisonment of women in Greek tragedy', *Journal of Hellenic Studies* 110 (1990), 76-90.

Vidal-Naquet, P., 'Sophocles' *Philoctetes* and the Ephebeia', in J.-P. Vernant and P. Vidal-Naquet *Myth and Tragedy in Ancient Greece* (English tr. J. Lloyd, Brighton 1981), 161-79.

Waldock, A.J.A., *Sophocles the Dramatist* (Cambridge 1951).

Wheeler, G., 'Gender and transgression in Sophocles' *Electra*', *Classical Quarterly* 53 (2003), 377-88.

Index